To: Jonathan

The 7 Seeds of Self-Transformation

Shakira Stuart
(Black Tea & Honey)

Dig Deep. Discover. Develop.

Words defined using:

Lexico Online Dictionary (n.d.), Oxford. https://www.lexico.com/

Merriam-Webster Online Dictionary (n.d.), Merriam-Webster. ` https://www.merriam-webster.com/

Dictionary.com (n.d.) https://www.dictionary.com/

Edited / Formatted by:

Passionate Words
Editing Services

Table of Contents

Acknowledgements

I want to extend love and gratitude to the following persons who contributed to the existence of this book:

My dear uncle, Anthony Stuart. His early departure from this earth gave me a new outlook on life and loss. It also strengthened my desire to be a better person and make each day above ground count.

Shadé Watson, my therapist, who has also become a mentor to me. She helped me to really understand myself and discover my true power and potential. She never hesitated to share difficult truths when I needed to hear them most.

Sarah Hubbard, my Meditation Instructor. She is such a sweet, gentle spirit. She didn't only teach me about meditation, she taught me so much about loving kindness and grace, simply by being a living example.

Together, they gave me the seeds that I planted to grow, and now share with you.

Robert Gibson of Passionate Words Editing Services. He was very encouraging and helpful from our very first conversation. He really stood by his client mantra, "I got you!" and I'm so grateful for that.

Family and friends that encouraged me to keep writing and exploring my talent. Special shout out to those that gave me feedback on excerpts and activities from the book while it was still in production.

Most importantly, the Higher Power that pushed me to keep going even when I felt lost and discouraged. It was very challenging at times but worth every minute and every effort invested.

Preface

I've sat in my therapist's chair and spilled my guts a countless number of times. I've also read too many self-help, personal development and spiritual books to count. I've journaled my thoughts and feelings until my fingers were sore. All of this work that I've poured into myself was not in vain, thankfully. I witnessed my own transformation over the past few years. It's been so evident that persons close to me often comment on how I've changed and how much they admire the "new me". Most of them never saw the tears, frustration and breakdowns, though. Currently, I'm still evolving, still learning and still transforming. Whenever I reflect on my journey so far, certain themes keep reappearing at the root of my transformation. Themes that persons often speak of but don't truly live by. I've decided that I can't wait for the perfect moment to share what I've learned. I'll always be a work in progress. The best teachers are still learning. And the perfect moment doesn't exist.

This book encompasses knowledge gained through therapy sessions, independent research, observation and conversation with others on their own self-transformation journeys. I pass on this knowledge, giving my perspective and sharing some of my personal stories, with the intention of accompanying others through their own transformation. I have a deep desire to see others improve and evolve. I want to see persons happy and thriving. But you can't do this without getting in touch with your inner world. You need to face your fears and self-limiting beliefs if you want to destroy them. You also need to see the greatness within you if you want to bring it to life. What I offer you is a tool to get this done. When it gets lonely and discouraging, I want my words to offer comfort and encouragement. When it feels confusing, I want that you find a paragraph or a sentence to help you gain some clarity. When you're rejoicing, I want you to know that I am rejoicing with you too.

We are all one. My growth is my brothers' and sisters' growth. As theirs is mine.

Self-transformation

Is a beautiful thing

If only you embrace it

There will be struggles

There will be difficulties

There will be roadblocks

There will be beauty

And opportunity

In each of these.

- Black Tea & Honey

Introduction

Transformation – a marked change in form, nature, or appearance *(Lexico Online Dictionary)*

Self-Transformation – a transforming of one's own thoughts, actions, or behaviour *(Merriam-Webster Online Dictionary)*

Self-Transformation *(for the context of this book)* – the process of intentionally and consciously reshaping yourself, through a series of thoughts and actions, that push you to grow and shed layers of your old self which no longer serve you. The result of successful self-transformation is the realization of your highest, most authentic self. *(Shakira Stuart)*

Key Points to Note

- *This process will look different for everyone*
- *There is no set timeframe*
- *Results will vary*
- *Gentle self-evaluation, rest and recovery are necessary throughout the process*
- *This process IS for the weak, if you are willing to work to discover your STRENGTH*

"God grant me the serenity to accept the people I cannot change, the courage to change the one I can, and the wisdom to know it's me." — Unknown

KEY QUESTIONS TO ASK YOURSELF BEFORE STEPPING INTO THE PROCESS OF SELF-TRANSFORMATION

- Do you see room for self-improvement and growth?
- Are you prepared to realize your highest self?
- Are you willing to put in the work to meet this version of you?
- Are you willing to discover and accept painful truths?
- Are you willing to make difficult changes?
- Are you willing to keep trying even after perceived failures?
- Are you willing to evaluate yourself lovingly, without bias and judgement?
- Are you ready to hold yourself accountable every step of the way?
- Do you have an idea of what your highest self looks like? Describe him/her.
- What would you call him/her?

Your readiness and willingness to go through the process is the first step of self-transformation.

Feel free to jot down your answers to the above questions in your journal/notebook.

Self-Transformation ~ The Idea

Most of us have an idea of what we want our life to look like. But how often do you think about what **YOU** would look like in this life that you imagine? What qualities do you have? Are you kind to yourself and to others? Are you helpful? Are you loving? Are you committed and hardworking? Do you treat all that you have been blessed with, with honour and respect? Are you a thankful person? Do you pay it forward?

In dreaming up your ideal life, you must be mindful of all the work that you need to put in to get there. It really all starts with you. You hold your future in your own hands. You have the ability to shape your life in remarkable ways. As soon as you become aware and accepting of this personal power, then you're on your way to owning it. Owning this power comes with a high level of responsibility and accountability. It is no easy feat, but **it is possible.** And I think that is all you need to remember while going through the ups and downs, the ebbs and flows, the highs and lows. **It is possible.** Your goals, your dreams, your deepest desires – they are all **possible.** You probably won't achieve them without hard work and sacrifice though. After all, they say that nothing worth having comes easy. What makes you think that you would be exempt from this rule?

In this technological age, so much information is at our fingertips. All you have to do is Google a simple question and you get an overwhelming number of websites showing content related to your search. Sometimes we are all tempted to Google something grand, hoping for a simple 1-2-3 formula for quick results.

"How to get rich?"

"How to get over heartbreak?"

"How to get them to fall in love with me?"

"How to be a better parent?"

"How to be happy?"

I won't lie by saying that you won't get some useful information and a heap of knowledge. It's all there. The secret is – **YOU** need to do the work. In going through the process, you see that the seemingly simple 1-2-3 formula, has so many hidden steps, crossroads and detours, that it can get overwhelming and exhausting. If I signed up for a 3-step program and then I discovered there was a 1(a), 1(b), 1(c), etc. I'd be discouraged too. Moreover, if I kept running into unexpected difficulties, it might further deter me from going forward because I went into it thinking that I only had a few simple steps to complete. This is what usually happens when we try to turn a complex but beautiful process, such as self-transformation, into a 3-step program. Perhaps, each step is just a general guide, but the intricacies and nuances of the process are for you to figure out. And guess what? You have the power to do that too!

For this reason, I will constantly reiterate and reinforce the need to put in the work while encouraging you in being gentle with yourself as you figure it out along the way. What "it" is depends on you and your unique journey. This is a lifetime of work! I am not here to sell dreams. I am here to sell you on pursuing your dreams. Remember, it's challenging. But it's also **possible**.

Self-Transformation ~ The Journey

Think of yourself as an artist. Also think of yourself as your biggest work of art – your masterpiece. This piece is unfinished. But it has so much potential to be everything that you imagine, or even more. Every day, as the artist, you sit on your stool, staring at the creation in front of you, studying it deeply. Some days you're in awe at how far you've come with this piece. Other days, you see that there's a lot more work to be done. You have new ideas. You have a bigger vision. Some days, you think that you should be further along, or maybe, that you're doing it wrong. But what can you compare it to, when you're working on something that is one of a kind? Some days, you feel passionate about your work of art. You add a bit of color here, cover over something there, and make a few more brush strokes, in hopes that the piece comes alive even more. Then, you stop and stare. You smile contentedly, with a twinkle in your eye, because you see the vision manifesting before your eyes. It feels surreal. But this is reality. You can touch your work and feel the bumps on the canvas. You see a few mistakes that you made along the way, but it still turned out surprisingly lovely. It makes the art stand out more. It's fascinating and liberating to see... to be.

This is what self-transformation looks like. There is no blueprint nor one size fits all. You are chartering your own path. Expect confusion, frustration and discouraging feelings. Also expect moments of contentment, euphoria and pleasant surprise. You are challenging and shifting yourself and your thoughts in ways that you haven't before. You are challenging the biggest enemy you've ever encountered. The enemy within you. That little voice that says, "You can't do it so stop trying." "You're not good enough to do that." "That's just how you are so it makes no sense trying to change it." "It would be easier if you just ... *(insert something mediocre here)*."

That voice in your head can take up so much space and be so forceful that it stomps on every hope and dream that you have, turning everything into useless mush. But there's hope. Every bit of knowledge that you gain and use to push yourself forward in your self-transformation process becomes a new weapon that you can use to defeat the enemy. And this is why it all starts within. This is all an internal battle. A long, grueling and sometimes *very bloody one* – metaphorically speaking, of course.

Think of all the qualities that you need to develop within yourself to achieve your goals. Close your eyes and imagine this version of you. Include as many details as possible in this vision. How do you walk? How do you talk? What's your personality like? For the purpose of this exercise, we will call this version of you your alter ego. Make it fun by giving them a name.

It might feel a bit ridiculous at first but creating and embodying an alter ego is a great way to step into your highest self. It's usually a more fearless and liberated version of you. But it is still... **YOU!** Embodying your alter ego shows that the qualities you dream of, are already deep inside of you. They are often masked by doubt and fear, but you can use your alter ego to bring them forward.

The practice of creating an alter ego is no new idea. Think about Peter Parker and Spider-Man, Clark Kent and Superman, Bruce Wayne and Batman. They are all "normal" characters with extraordinary alter egos. Your alter ego doesn't have to be a crimefighting superhero though! You can be extraordinary in whatever way you choose. Think about Christina Aguilera and her alter ego Xtina. Mariah Carey and Mimi. Eminem and Slim Shady. Beyoncé and Sasha Fierce. Each of these celebrities created an alter ego which embodied another side of them – a bolder and more free-spirited side. Does creating an alter ego seem a little less strange now?

Think about it. You can be a receptionist by day but sing your heart out at bars and clubs at night. You can be a plumber during the week but an adventurer on weekends, discovering and exploring new places. Or in my case, you can be a Sales Assistant from 9 – 5 during the week but an author, life coach and self-love advocate outside of those hours. The world is your oyster! The aim is to step outside of the box that you created for yourself and be the person you really want to be. Do the things that you really want to do. Do the things that you call silly. Do the things that you think you'd fail at if you tried. Do the things that you love but you don't think you're very good at. Delve into the depths of your dreams, hobbies and anything else that will bring you happiness in this lifetime. There is more than one side to your character. The side that dominates is usually the one that you feel is most presentable and socially accepted. This is also the side that might be more reluctant to make mistakes, take risks and look completely insane. But how else do you truly learn and grow? Channel your alter ego to kickstart a new level of growth.

Let your alter ego become the artist. Let that side of you add a few details to your master creation. Your self-transformation cannot truly take place if you don't get out of your head and loosen the restraints that you placed on yourself. Years of conditioning, doubt and negative self-talk can really imprison your mind. But you also hold the key to release yourself and meet freedom. It's in your hands. The worst thing that you can do with your power is give it away, then wait for chance or luck to get you where you want to be.

Self-Transformation

- The 7 Seeds

You thought of yourself as an artist working on a masterpiece.

Now think of yourself as a plot of land with great potential to turn into a beautiful garden. There's a great mix of sunlight and rainfall. The soil is extremely fertile. The land is promising. Everything looks right. You're also the farmer. You are responsible for planting the seeds and taking care of the garden so that you reap bountiful crops to feed yourself and those around you. You have a mighty job. If you succeed, you and everyone that you share with will be well fed. With the strength from those meals and the knowledge that you pass on in farming, they too can make use of their land and feed themselves and others to come. It is a cycle. We sow the seeds and reap the crops. We share the crops with others so that they can repeat the process. If you don't succeed, not only will you suffer, but you'll also cause the suffering of those around you. Their dependents, in turn, suffer too. Until someone breaks the cycle and turns it all around, the suffering will continue to spread.

This is how life works. All of us are interconnected and rely on others in some way. Your first responsibility is you. You have to start by working on your own garden before you can help anyone else with theirs. Those closest to you are affected by the work that you put into yourself. Positive thought and action reap positive results in your life and the lives of those you influence – family, friends, colleagues, etc. Similarly, negative action reaps negative results in your life and the lives of those you influence. Now here's the tricky part: perceived negative thought does not have to lead to negative action. It's all about how you choose to handle these thoughts.

If you preach, and more importantly, practice love and kindness, those around you will feel that energy and even if they don't return it in the moment, they will be taking in subconscious lessons from your actions towards them. If you have hateful or hurtful thoughts you can choose to explore these feelings, get to the root of them and heal yourself. Alternatively, you can choose to allow them to lead you to constantly say and do hateful and hurtful things. If you do go this route, that is the energy that you are putting out into the universe. That is the energy that those around you will feel. That is the energy that those around you will sometimes reciprocate and pass on. That is the energy that will eventually surround you.

Let's use a simple example. You had a bad day at work. You made a huge mistake that will potentially cost you an important client.

You reach home and start arguing with your partner over something silly because you're in a bad space mentally. They forgot to fold the laundry and take out the garbage. Normally, this would be no big deal but you're already really on edge. You don't know how to address and release your anger and disappointment with yourself in a healthy way. You find yourself shouting and insulting your partner, unable to calm down. They get defensive and return the same energy. They have no idea what happened at work, but they feel attacked by you. You guys don't speak for the rest of the night. The next morning your partner is still thinking about the argument. They're agitated and distracted at work. A workmate approaches them and makes a joke, which your partner takes the wrong way. They lash out at their workmate, who in turn feels that it was an overreaction and they're hurt by how things unfolded. It is that easy for your energetic vibrations to be passed on. Not only did you suffer, but you also caused the suffering of someone around you and then by extension, someone around them. Of course, your partner could have ended the cycle. But it doesn't take away from the fact that it started with you. You have the power to determine what energy you put out. You have the power to determine what seeds you plant. You have the power to determine how you will care for these seeds as they grow. You have the power to determine what your garden will look like. You have the power to feed yourself and those around you. It is a lot of power and responsibility and it is all yours.

After much deliberation and contemplation, I decided on 7 seeds for self-transformation. I believe that the first fruit that you bear should come from these seeds. Stepping into your highest self, your fearless and liberated alter ego, requires a careful understanding of these before you plant them. I believe that by planting these seeds and caring for them diligently, your yield will be immense. Dare I say, you cannot experience the full bloom of that beautiful garden without these 7 seeds. Studying and living by these 7 concepts will help you to unlock your true potential and see the life that you live through new eyes. These 7 seeds serve as a guiding light throughout your transformation.

They are:

- Awareness
- Acceptance
- Gratitude
- Love
- Faith
- Patience
- Discipline

Awareness

Awareness – Knowledge or perception of a situation or fact *(Lexico Online Dictionary)*

Self-awareness – Conscious knowledge of one's own character, feelings, motives, and desires *(Lexico Online Dictionary)*

Self-awareness *(for the context of this book)* – Your knowledge and understanding of yourself and your inner world, including your thoughts, feelings, intentions, impulses and resulting behaviours *(Shakira Stuart)*

I remember when I was a slave.

Not in the physical sense.

But I was a slave.

I was so mentally and emotionally imprisoned.

All the while unaware.

I could not free myself from this jail.

Because I knew not that I was there.

The very things that held me captive.

I thought they gave me freedom.

My unconscious actions.

My reckless thoughts.

Locked me further away.

Like Fort Knox.

I was a slave to my own emotions.

I was a slave to others' opinions.

I was a slave to the wrath of my lover.

All I did was suffer...

And suffer...

But there was no escape.

As I was unaware of these very restraints.

- Black Tea & Honey

The Foundation - Awareness of Self

Your self-awareness is the foundation of your self-transformation. It is the first building stone which the entire process relies heavily on. As such, do not take it lightly.

Before you take on the task of accepting, changing or learning to work with something, you should first have that awareness of what it is and what it entails. This same concept applies when that something that you are working on is you. Gaining that clarity about who you are and what you want out of life is empowering, giving you the confidence to make positive changes. Like with all the other seeds that I will be planting in this book, you have to work your way from the inside out. Start with self-awareness, then build your awareness of everything else around you – persons, situations, circumstances, etc.

After going through this process myself, I can safely say this – If you do not develop a certain level of self-awareness, you will always be a slave. You will be easily influenced, confused, reactive and feel powerless very often. Life will just be happening to you. You will put yourself through unnecessary pain by being disconnected from your inner world.

A lot of people tend to spend so much time trying to fix others and situations. That time can be so wisely spent on your own development. I am surely speaking from experience here. I was part of this collective. When I realized what I was doing, then I was able to start to work on reducing the occurrence of this habit, until I completely quit. Did you notice my first step? Awareness. I became cognizant of what I was unconsciously doing out of habit, that it wasn't working for me and most importantly, that it was very unhealthy, so I needed to stop. I'll paint a picture...

I was in a relationship with a partner who constantly mistreated me. He was disrespectful, manipulative and gaslit me whenever I tried to bring up issues with his behaviour. I'd tell him that I didn't appreciate how he spoke to me and he would react by lashing out at me and telling me that I was too sensitive. He became very angry during confrontations, throwing stuff and punching walls. I kept looking for different ways to approach the issue. Every single approach backfired. I was also praying that he would change. I remember saying to myself, "This relationship could work if he just..." I felt powerless in the situation. Eventually, I began to believe that I was actually too sensitive. I normalized his toxic and emotionally abusive behaviour. The relationship ended before I began to work on my self-awareness. He was the one that broke it off. So, I spent a lot of time beating myself up and wishing that the situation was different.

After some soul searching and many therapy sessions, I realized that I had the power to walk away from the situation all along. I didn't want to own this power because I didn't want to deal with the pain and hurt of the breakup. In the end, I still had to deal with the very pain that I was avoiding. Life is funny like that. If I knew myself then, he wouldn't have been able to convince me that I was too sensitive. If I were more aware then, I would have realized that the person that I wanted him to be simply did not exist in that moment. That was the reality of the situation. Maybe he had the potential to become the person that I envisioned, but it was for him to realize his potential. It was all on him to change if he wanted to. That was not my task to take on. I could only choose whether or not I wanted to be with him as he was.

Situations like this played out in many other areas in my life – with family, with friends, with my boss. When there is a lesson to be learnt, the more you try to avoid it, the more often it will appear. Awareness was a big lesson for me. I came to realize that you do what you can based on what you know. Don't ignore the signs and the lessons. When you know better, do better!

I want better for you and for everyone out there really. So, I'll go even deeper into how you can build your level of awareness.

ACTIVITY: Who Am I? – Awareness of Self

Have you ever asked yourself the question "Who am I?"

Can you answer this question confidently? Who are you, really?

Take away all the external factors and talk about yourself alone. Don't mention your job, your family, your friends, your studies, your possessions nor your successes. Who are you at your very core? This is a great self-reflection exercise, so feel free to bring out that journal again! Focusing on yourself can sometimes feel so overwhelming because there are so many layers to peel back and explore. Sometimes you don't know where, when and how to start. Well right here, right now, using this exercise is a great place to begin your self-exploration. Sit with yourself. Be quiet. Turn off the distractions. Answer the below questions as best as you can.

Who are you?

What are your strengths?

What are your weaknesses?

What makes you happy? And why?

What offends you? And why?

What makes you sad? And why?

What are your values?

What are your goals and dreams?

Are you already working towards them? If not, then why?

Where do you see yourself in 5 years?

You can revisit this exercise as many times as you need to. I promise you that there is something beautiful for you to discover. Only when you delve into the depths of yourself can you truly build on your strengths, be mindful of the "why" behind your actions, see what you want to change, trust your intuition, and understand your own emotions and feelings. You can really become a powerhouse and a force to be reckoned with, by just knowing who you really are.

This is such a deep, long and intricate process though. It is okay to do more research, speak with a friend or even book a therapy session. Any work that you're doing on yourself is worth doing.

What Power Do I Have? My Circle of Control

A deep sense of empowerment. Inner strength. Unbreakable confidence.

I see that for you!

I want that for you!

It looks great on you!

Your personal power is a strength that you might often overlook. That mental toughness and tenacity that you bring to situations. The ability to take decisive and deliberate action. The process of working through uncomfortable feelings and situations, while remaining focused on the goal ahead. All of that is power that you own. To be fully aware of that power and how to utilize it is not a skill that many hone though.

Focusing on the things that you cannot control is sometimes the root of feeling powerless. Although this is the case, people tend to focus so much more on the outer world than what's going on inside them. This happens because there's so much to do and so much going on that it is hard to disconnect. So many things around you demand your attention. It can be your family, your friends, your home, your job, your pets, your hobbies – it's an inexhaustible list, really. What makes it even more consuming is that nothing is ever perfect! There's always something that you want to change, improve or maybe even completely get rid of or build from scratch. So, getting caught up in the chaos around you is almost an automatic response. You have an attachment to the people and things around you and that's okay. But most of these things that you're so fixated on, you have little to no control over. Let's face it, sometimes shit happens! You might take the best care of your house, but a hurricane could completely destroy it. You could try to be the most loving and encouraging partner, but your spouse could be ungrateful and not reciprocate this energy. You could go above and beyond every day at work and still lose your job because the company needed to downsize. You could be the shoulder to lean on for your best-friend, showing up for them a countless amount of times, and the one time you didn't, they could get mad and claim that you're never there for them. Now, I am not saying that you shouldn't always do your best. I am saying that even if you do your best, a situation may not spin in your favour. Or so it may seem in that moment. Stay with me here. Especially when life goes haywire, you have to shift your focus to what you can control.

So, let's focus on the things in your control instead. What is within your circle of control? Do you know what is the first, the last, and the only thing on the list? I'm hoping that you guessed it correctly. The answer is **YOU**. That's why self-awareness is so important. It focuses on something that you have control over and can change if you wanted to. Your personal power allows you to live a more intentional life with a sense of purpose. It allows you to effectively manage your boundaries. It allows you to work on breaking destructive thought patterns and habits. There's even a theory about it! It's called the Self-Awareness Theory and has been around for several decades. It was developed by Duval and Wicklund in their book called "A Theory of Objective Self-Awareness." It explains that you are not your thoughts, but the entity observing your thoughts. You are the thinker, separate and apart from the thoughts. You are consciousness. You are awareness. You observe your emotions, feelings and actions. Your awareness notices when you're sad. It notices when you're uncomfortable. It notices when you're happy. It notices that you're reading these words right now and trying to make sense of what I'm saying. Whether you consciously tap into that awareness or not, it's always hard at work, observing and analyzing all that is going on around and within you. If you don't channel that energy, your awareness tends to become too focused on what's going on around, and neglect within.

With Great Awareness Comes Great Accountability

Would you consider yourself to be self-aware?

Do you really hold yourself accountable?

Do you focus on your circle of control?

Let's look at a scenario. You work a very demanding job and you have a strained relationship with your boss. Actually, the relationship is pretty horrible. Your boss never notices your efforts. She talks down on you and belittles you in team meetings, she chastises you for the smallest mistakes and she never wants to hear what you have to say. At first, you tried to work harder, hoping that she would see that you're an asset to the team. Over time, you get frustrated and you decide to fight fire with fire. When she is rude, you're rude right back! She deserves it! You stop putting in as much effort because she doesn't appreciate it anyway. Every time you see her your blood boils and your body tenses. You've stopped interacting with her outside of work-related conversations. You hope that she notices that you no longer have much to say to her. You become accustomed to her behaviour and you match her energy because you don't tolerate disrespect. This is the new normal for you. You become accustomed to this unhealthy relationship. You dread work every day and avoid interactions with her. Whenever you two do interact, it's hostile or indifferent.

This situation sounds draining. But believe it or not, so many persons have similar relationships with a boss, a parent, a sibling, a colleague, a partner. Going tic for tac and hurting each other continuously. Because it is a common occurrence, doesn't mean it is right. Think about this situation and how you would go about dealing with it. Be honest with yourself.

Now it's so easy to play the Blame Game.

"I only did "xyz" because of what they did first."

"They made me retaliate that way."

This doesn't align with the concept of owning your personal power. If you are fully tapped into the power that you have, no one can MAKE you react a certain way. Your feelings, how you react to situations, the effort that you put in, how you take care of yourself, your decisions are all within your control. You can have big feelings but don't let them consume you. Honour and release in a healthy way. Instead of worsening the relationship with your boss, you can choose to hold yourself accountable. It can go something like this.

"My boss is mean and disrespectful. I cannot control her words and actions. But I can control mine. I choose to respond respectfully each time, even if it is difficult for me."

"I notice tension in my body whenever my boss is nearby. I choose to find methods to release this tension so that I am not negatively affected by her presence. It's for my own good."

"My boss doesn't seem to want to change the nature of our relationship. I choose to go about this differently. I choose to communicate my frustrations in a respectful manner. I'll call a meeting with her and then with her and HR if necessary, so that we can work on this issue."

"However this situation spins, I choose to honour my feelings and find peace. My peace is more important to me than proving that I am right or getting back at her."

Handling difficult situations in this way will be uncomfortable. It will be challenging. You're rewiring your mind to think a different way and take a different path. Don't expect to get it right the first time. Maybe not even the tenth. The secret to the self-accountability sauce is to **keep trying**. That's probably the secret to life's sauce as well, but I digress.

Keep checking in with yourself. Keep focusing on what you can control and how you will control it. Keep reminding yourself that you hold the power to how you handle situations in your life. Even if you're not responsible for the situation, you're responsible for how you respond to it. Choose peace.

ACTIVITY: A Commitment to Inner Self

To further your self-awareness and work on mastering your circle of control, I will need you to make a commitment to yourself.

How often do you absentmindedly check your phone? Or maybe just grab it to scroll through social media aimlessly? Think about it for a moment and be honest with yourself. No judgement here.

You're standing in the grocery line and about 3 persons are ahead of you, so you pull out your phone to kill the time. You just finished work and it was a long day. You flop down on the couch and decide to relax for a few minutes so that you can clear your mind. You pick up your phone to see what you missed while you were busy, and you end up spending an hour on social media. You wake up in the morning and you're ready to start your day. You grab your phone to answer any messages, check emails and social media accounts. You see an important message from a client and then your day kicks into full swing from there.

It's so easy to get lost in the technological world. It's part of your work. It's part of your studies. It's part of your entertainment. It's also one of your distractions. But when do you decide that it's too much? When do you decide that it is taking away from your inner work? I challenge you to schedule social media time each day. Maybe one hour a day? Or break it down into four 15-minute sessions spread across the day. Maybe you're on social media so much that you need to slowly wean yourself off. So, you may need to start with 2 hours a day. That's okay. Figure out what works for you. But hold yourself accountable. You will absentmindedly grab for your phone often the first few days or weeks. That's okay too. You're breaking a habit. Stop yourself whenever you reach for your phone outside of the scheduled time and without having an important reason to use it. Instead, challenge yourself further by doing what I will call an *"Inner Self Check"* Exercise.

- **Take 5 deep breaths**
- **Close your eyes (optional) and ask yourself these questions:**
  - **What am I feeling right now?**
  - **Have I been honouring my emotions, or have I been suppressing them?**
  - **Am I fully present or is something else on my mind?**
  - **Is this something within my control or am I worrying without perspective?**
  - **How can I be kinder to myself?**
- **Open your eyes and spend a few seconds observing any**

feelings/sensations in your body

This exercise also works well when you are trying to process uncomfortable emotions or when you're working through a difficult situation. The aim is to become more acquainted with how you feel and what you need to give to yourself in that moment. Instead of running from discomfort or perceived negative emotions, take your time and explore those feelings. After all, they're just feelings. Trade in any unhealthy coping mechanisms (such as alcohol, drugs, sex or overeating, for example) and try the Inner Self Check instead.

Become more aware of your thought patterns and how they may be guiding you. Take control of yourself in difficult situations and assess your personal power and how you're going to use it. Your thoughts and feelings in any situation are simply there to tell you what's going on in your inner world, and how the outer world is affecting you. Embrace them!

In the words of Sadhguru, Indian yogi, mystic and visionary, *"Don't try to stop negative thoughts, as there is no such thing as a positive or negative thought. Fighting your thoughts is like fighting your own ghosts – you make them and then fight against them. If you win, then you've really lost it!"*

Acceptance

Acceptance - the act of taking or receiving something offered *(Dictionary.com)*

Acceptance *(for the context of this book)* - willingness to see and embrace the truth within you and the truth that surrounds you, whether it is perceived as a positive or a negative truth *(Shakira Stuart)*

Sometimes things change

When you don't want them to

Sometimes it feels too soon

So fleeting

You didn't even get a chance

To embrace the feeling

You feel wronged

Unfaired

Disfavoured

Why is the world so unkind?

Now you're confused

Frustrated

Stuck & tongue-tied

The natural flow of life

Becomes your riptide

It feels like you're drowning

Until you open your eyes

To the very nature of being

Now you realize

That growth and grace

Is ACCEPTING it for what it is

To relieve yourself of suffering

You breathe deeply and lean in

Letting go of

That unconscious need to resist

Lean in, my love

Only then can you rise above

- Black Tea & Honey

Unconditional Acceptance

With great awareness comes the challenge of acceptance.

I know what you're thinking.

"Another challenge?"

"The deeper I go, the more there is to uncover."

Or maybe I'm completely wrong and you're enjoying the journey so far.

Regardless of whether you're experiencing some joy in this journey or not, you're still here and that's a good sign. It shows your commitment to, or – at the very least – your interest in this process. It shows your willingness to acquire new knowledge for your own self-development. It shows that something is resonating with you. It's keeping you going. And really, that small effort at the beginning is all you need to build the momentum. It's all you need to complete your first step towards your own improvement.

Now that you have delved into awareness and discovered new things about yourself and all that surrounds you, acceptance comes into play. You might wonder how. You realize all these things about your thoughts, your behaviours and your actions. You also realize so many things about persons and situations in your life that cause friction. Just because you become aware, doesn't mean that you automatically accept. Sometimes, our first response is to resist when we encounter something that we perceive as negative. Who wants to embrace something undesirable with open arms anyway? Well, does it sound crazy to recommend that you do? Arthur Rubinstein, one of the greatest pianists of the 20th century, once said, *"Of course there is no formula for success except, perhaps, an unconditional acceptance of life and what it brings."* Could you imagine accepting everything that is thrown at you as it comes? Just going with the flow and letting things unfold as they will anyway? The concept sounded absurd to me when I first heard it too. But there's method to the madness!

Answer the following questions honestly. This is another great journal exercise. It's okay if your answer to some or even all the questions is "No". This is a safe space. Absolutely no judgement. That's correct, you shouldn't be judging yourself here. Non-judgmental observation is key.

Do you accept yourself just as you are?

Do you accept the uncomfortable feelings that arise when you do your Inner Self Checks?

Do you accept your power?

Do you accept the situations that you CAN'T change?

Do you accept the situations that you CAN change?

ACTIVITY: Do You Truly Accept Yourself? Flaws and All?

I want you to take a few minutes to look at yourself in the mirror. I mean truly look at yourself. This is called the **Reflection Exercise**. This will be a very vulnerable moment. Strip completely naked and meet your full reflection in the mirror. Look into your own eyes. Pay attention to the shape and contours of your face. Run your fingers over any scars or pimples. Let your gaze fall to your body. Observe its full shape. Observe the marks, dimples and pimples there too. Look at each limb. Look at your torso. Look at every single part of your body that you're able to get a good view of. Allow the discomfort to arise. It will come. Now start to think about your inner self. The parts that you can't see. Your mind. Your heart. Your character. Think about your strengths, weaknesses, successes and failures. Think of the ways you've grown or changed as time went by. Again, allow the discomfort to arise. Sit with it. Maybe you feel like you're the best version of yourself right now. Or maybe there's an older version of you that you prefer, and you still mourn. Whatever thoughts come to your mind during this exercise, let them in without resistance. Journal these thoughts. Don't try to sugar-coat nor water them down either. Keep them as raw and unfiltered as possible. It's important to see in writing how you really feel about yourself in this moment. Read it over a few times.

This exercise is critical to your self-awareness and self-acceptance.

However, some people won't be able to complete it. Truly looking at yourself and facing the thoughts you have about you is a heavy task. But it is a necessary one. Remember, awareness and acceptance of self is the goal! That's why you need to be totally honest in this exercise. If you pretend that everything is all good, then you'll never see what you need to work on. I am challenging you to open a vault that persons often keep locked. It's scary in there, I know. But it also unlocks another level of personal power and a type of sovereignty that you'll only understand once you experience it. We're turning the autopilot off and taking control with this one. I want you to experience self-acceptance in its purest form at some point during your journey.

If someone asks, "Do you accept yourself?" Your reply might be an automatic yes. Of course, you do. Why wouldn't you? Or of course, you should. So, you feel compelled to answer yes. But if you really, wholeheartedly, unconditionally accept yourself, then why do you speak negatively to yourself on so many occasions? Why do you despise the things in you that you see as weakness? Why do you fixate on all the flaws in your image and stress about how much you'd like to change them? Why do you hide the parts of yourself that you don't like? Why do you feel guilty and ashamed when your thoughts or actions are not what you think they should be? Why do you keep replaying your mistakes and beating yourself to a pulp for what has already happened? Why do you automatically look for the shortcomings in moments when you should be celebrating your success? Why do you constantly feel like you're not doing enough? Why do you feel like **you're** not enough?

Well, I told you to be honest so it's only fair that I am too. That's not self-acceptance. Self-acceptance isn't conditional. Free yourself from your harsh inner critic. Free yourself from that nagging voice that always says "But..." when you try to focus on the good. Invite grace and compassion in instead. It's easy to accept whatever you perceive as positive and pleasing. Your loyalty to your friends, your generosity, your creative nature. Whatever it may be. You'll seldom have trouble embracing it if you see it as a positive aspect of yourself. But the ones that you perceive as negative? You may struggle with accepting *those*. Your lack of dedication, your fear of taking chances, all the goals that you set but didn't even try to achieve. Contrary to popular habit, beating yourself up, wishing you were different and rejecting parts of yourself that you don't like will not help you to do and become better. Instead, it will just slow down your progress and maybe even lead to depression, anxiety and a whole other host of mental issues, if your self-loathing runs that deep. Let's nip it in the bud before it gets any worse.

This leads us into another exercise linked to the Reflection Exercise. Once again, read over what you wrote during your self-analysis in the mirror. This one is called the **Reset Exercise**. The aim is to reset the thoughts that you have about yourself by replacing negative ones with positive ones. You'll do this by using **affirmations**.

If this is the first time that you're hearing about affirmations, they are basically powerful statements used to challenge negative and self-sabotaging thoughts. Using affirmations, you will consciously redirect your thoughts and overtime reprogram your mind, helping to create a new belief system in the area that you target. Affirmations are short, positive and written in the present tense. You're speaking it as if it already is, therefore, calling it to be. You can use affirmations as often as you'd like.

Now, back to the exercise! Highlight the negative things that you would have written about yourself. You have to come up with affirmations for at least three of the negative things you would have stated. A lot of the time, that negativity that you feed yourself is without context. For example, a new mom might have negative thoughts about her body, conscious of the fact that she just had a baby, but still not really understanding and fully embracing that it's okay that her body has changed because she just birthed an entire human. So, her affirmations for body positivity might look like this.

"I love my body."

"My body is strong."

"My body is allowed to change."

"I am grateful for all that my body has done."

"I make healthy choices for my body rooted in love."

I'll give another example to expand your thoughts even more. Let's say that you've been struggling mentally for the past few months and, as a result, you haven't been very productive. No matter what you tried, you couldn't bring your mind to focus for long periods of time. You generally felt demotivated and empty, so you closed your business for a few days. Then you started to feel guilty about it and your negative self-talk looked like "I'm so lazy. I should be productive. I hate that I can't beat this feeling. I shouldn't be taking such a long break. I need to get back to work and forget about how I feel. I just want to feel normal again." During your negative self-talks, you're not considering that you've been working for the past year and a half without a vacation. You're also not considering that you've been arguing with your spouse a lot lately and this has also been draining your energy.

Your affirmations might look like this.

"I deserve rest and recovery."

"My mental health is a priority."

"I love myself enough to take breaks when I need them."

"I honour my feelings and I am patient with myself."

"I take breaks so that I return reenergized."

These affirmations won't work right away. But they will ease some of the guilt and sadness. When paired with other self-improvement exercises, they work wonders! They help you to feel better about yourself, which in turn affects your actions and habits.

Once you come up with your affirmations, return to the mirror and recite them out loud. Really feel and embrace each word that you speak. Congratulate yourself for completing the exercise. Revisit your affirmations daily. For that extra push, you can even write or print them out and place them somewhere in your space that you frequent. Personally, I found that right above my bathroom mirror was ideal. I'd read over my affirmations while completing mundane tasks like brushing my teeth or fixing my hair.

Accepting What You CANNOT Change

So, you've looked at yourself and you're working on true self-acceptance. But what about everything around you? All those things that you have no control over? Things that you wish you could change although you have absolutely no power to do so? Well, there's one thing that you can change when you look at those things – your mindset and your perspective. It's not so much the thing – the situation, the person, the place – that's the issue. It's your attitude and feelings towards it. A thing is just that – a thing. We are the ones who decide if that thing is negative or positive based on how we feel about it. Something as serious as death, for example, is just another thing in life. Every death in the world doesn't directly affect us. We know that death is inevitable, so we won't mourn every time we hear of a death. But it's different when it's someone that is close to us. It is how we feel about the death of that loved one that really makes it difficult.

There's a well-known Taoist story that really helps us to see that it is all about our interpretation, more so than the actual reality. Our interpretation shapes our personal reality, really. When our interpretation changes, our reality changes with it. In the story, there's an older farmer who had worked his crops for many years. One day his horse ran away. His neighbours came to visit when they heard the news. They all offered words of comfort and stated that what had happened was such bad luck. However, lo and behold, the next morning, the horse returned with three other wild horses. The neighbours were happy for the old man now. "How wonderful!" they exclaimed. The following day, while trying to ride one of the untamed horses, the farmer's son fell and broke his leg. The neighbours once again came by and offered their sympathy on his misfortune. The day after, military officials came to the village to draft young men into the army. Seeing that the son's leg was broken, they did not draft him. The neighbours heard this news and congratulated the farmer on how well things had turned out for him and his son.

Each time the neighbors commented about the old man's good luck or misfortune, his only reply was a calm and cool "Maybe." Maybe the old man knew what I now know. Maybe the old man knew what I'm now teaching you. In the moment, you may feel like something is such a bad thing. It stirs up all types of uncomfortable emotions inside you that are difficult to deal with. So, you call the situation a negative one. You reject whatever it is, because in your mind, that's not how it should be. But you know what? It is attachment and resistance to change that is often the root of human suffering. And our resistance comes from our attachment to how we think things should or could be, or maybe our longing for things to be how they were.

Think about it. Why do you feel so sad for so long after a breakup? You don't want things to change. You miss how things were with that person. You've become so accustomed to their presence in your life. You don't like the "new normal" without them. Maybe, you're even still clinging to them long after your journey together ended. You miss the way they made you feel.

Fast forward to a few months later. You're in a way better place mentally and emotionally. You're adjusting to and ENJOYING single life. You're finding and embracing joy where you can. You're getting reacquainted with yourself. You didn't realize how much you neglected yourself while pouring into the relationship. Now, you're making the most of this time alone and focusing on you.

Essentially, do you know what you did there? You ACCEPTED the breakup and the absence of that person playing that role in your life. You ACCEPTED change. Only through acceptance were you able to embrace and get the most out of this change. Then, you start to see that maybe the breakup wasn't such a bad thing after all. It just felt that way at the time. This can be applied to almost anything in life – losing a loved one, losing your job, relocating to a whole new country. Life is fluid. Change is constant. Acceptance is a necessary tool if you want to move with the eb and flow of life.

You don't have to rush acceptance but be mindful that it lays the foundation for adjustment and moving on. Give yourself time to grieve the loss of whatever or whoever you have to move on without. Feel sadness, emptiness, anger, even denial. This is all a necessary part of the process, especially if the situation is extremely difficult. The key is to know that you won't stay in this place. You will adjust and overcome. Plant the seed of acceptance early on, so that it can flow through you freely once you've processed all those heavy emotions.

Accepting What You CAN Change

There's so much focus on accepting the things you cannot change. Even the popular Serenity Prayer says *"God, grant me the serenity to accept the things I cannot change, courage to change the things*

I can, and wisdom to know the difference." This is a prayer I've recited many times, especially while going through difficulties. One day, I studied the prayer, reading it over and over and letting each word digest slowly in my mind. I remember asking myself why am I only accepting the things that I cannot change? Does acceptance of something automatically mean that I do not intend to change it? So why do they tell us to accept our flaws, even if we are working on them? Perhaps, this is one of the fundamental issues with acceptance and how it is taught. Perhaps, this is why we struggle to accept certain things about ourselves, knowing that we have the potential to change or improve. After these series of thoughts, I just couldn't see the prayer the same way. I still love it and see its power, but if I were to tweak it, I'd say *"God, grant me the serenity* **to accept ALL things as they are**, *the wisdom to know which of these things I can change, and the courage to make those changes."*

Let's revisit the circle of control. Do you remember the focus of your circle of control? That's right - YOURSELF! Wouldn't it be a contradiction to ask you to accept yourself unconditionally but also ask you to only accept the things you cannot change? Let's say that you tend to be lazy and disorganized. You have big goals and you know that you can do better but you're not there yet. You're struggling with breaking this habit. Should you ridicule and reject that aspect of you because you know that you can do better? No! Healthy change is built on a solid foundation of self-love, self-compassion, gentleness, and self-acceptance. You don't bash and beat yourself into becoming a better person. Instead, you make the efforts to understand and accept where you're at in this particular stage in your life. You also make a commitment to work on what you've accepted and, also want to improve on. The two can and they do go hand in hand. This is the best way to approach change. The "why" behind your actions is as important as the action itself. You don't want to make changes rooted in self-loathing but, instead, out of a genuine desire to be a better version of yourself. Your intentions behind your actions will dictate the way you talk to yourself, the approaches that you take and the way that you bounce back when you fall off. If it is rooted in self-loathing, chances are progress will be slow and your actions will be counter-productive. If it is rooted in self-compassion and acceptance, then you have a real chance to flourish.

Why Acceptance Before Action?

Imagine wanting to make a change. Imagine wanting to make this change without accepting the reality of the situation as it is in that moment. The opposite of acceptance is denial, refusal or rejection. Imagine being in denial about this thing that deeply impacts something that you want to change. What do you think will happen? How successful do you think you'll be in making that change?

To paint a clearer picture, let's explore this situation together. Imagine that you just reached home from the doctor. The doctor told you that you're obese and you have high blood pressure. You need to work on your eating habits and increase your activity as soon as possible. The doctor confirmed what you already knew. You've been beating yourself up about this for months now. You've started many diet programs, but you never saw them through. You know deep down inside that you overeat to comfort yourself and cope with stress. This is confirmed by your recent weight gain as things became more stressful with an important project you've been working on. Although you were able to see that you were stress eating, you rejected this fact, calling it a stupid excuse. That's not a valid reason to overeat. No one should overeat, no matter how they are feeling. You've been saying this to yourself over and over. You're in denial about how much food comforts you and makes you feel better. You're in denial about your reason for overeating being valid. It's hard to make real changes when you won't even accept your relationship with food. You find the behaviour disgusting but you can't manage to stop indulging.

The truth is, living a healthy lifestyle is hard. Most of us won't be able to keep up with it 24/7. You first accept that food is your comfort. Your reason is valid. Your feelings are valid too. It is okay to want and sometimes need comfort. You're only human. Once you can accept this, you can look at other ways to comfort yourself.

Maybe get into journaling, painting, yoga or watch reruns of your favourite show. You can even look for healthy foods that you enjoy as an alternative. You can thank yourself for finding ways to self-soothe during difficult times. They might not have been ideal, but you did the best you could at the time. It's okay to be gentle with yourself even though you've made mistakes or did things that you want to change. Maybe you can also look for other ways to detach from the stresses of your life. Take a walk in nature, see a therapist, try meditation.

It will be much easier to see things through and pick yourself back up when you fall, once you adopt a mindset of acceptance. You don't need to "fix" your thoughts and feelings by rejecting them. You accept them, even though you might see them as "bad". Then you lovingly open yourself up to another perspective. You move intentionally, but also with patience and grace. This is why acceptance before action is so important. Only through honest observation and acceptance, can you properly strategize how to move forward. You want to make meaningful, long-term changes out of love for and commitment to yourself and your growth.

Gratitude

Gratitude - The quality of being thankful; readiness to show appreciation for and to return kindness *(Lexico Online Dictionary)*

Gratitude *(for the context of this book)* – a deep feeling of appreciation for something expressed through thought, words and action *(Shakira Stuart)*

You see

Life is simpler than you think

When you realize it can all change in a blink

Of an eye, a split second, a flash, a heartbeat

That's all it takes to change an entire reality

Don't you know we are so temporary?

Nothing but specks of dust

Nothing promised to us

But this moment

Here and now

Do you cherish the present?

Or spend it anyhow?

Do you smile when you take in a breath of fresh air?

Do you go outdoors just to stop and stare?

At the gift that is given unto you?

You can see

You can hear

You can hug your loved ones

And let them know that you care

Do you tell your friends thank you

For simply being there?

Do you embrace the comfort of soft sheets on your skin?

Do you love all others with your entire being?

Don't hold back

There's no later

There's nothing greater

Than this very moment

So why not live it with intent?

Spend a whole day at the beach

With the waves crashing at your feet

Sipping on your favourite tea

Or maybe a fruit smoothie

Or wine

Or whiskey

Then listen to your lover's heartbeat

Life is as sweet as we want it to be

Just an ounce of gratitude

Makes it an even more satisfying treat

It's just the moment

It's all we're sure to see

It's on you to live it wholeheartedly

Before that moment becomes a memory

- Black Tea & Honey

Gratitude – What Does It Feel Like?

One morning, I was at the kitchen sink of my upstairs apartment washing my mug. It was an ordinary day as I started it the same way. I had just finished up my meditation and recital of affirmations, and I was preparing to have some tea. As I was rinsing out the last bit of suds from the mug, I looked through the window. The first thing that caught my eye was a sheep with her little lamb closely in tow on the pasture next to the apartment. Sheep are usually grazing there during the day, once the weather permits. But this day felt particularly different. The breeze was blowing, and I could see the tall grass and leaves of the surrounding trees dancing in sync. The colors of the grass and the morning sky seemed magnified. Everything had a brightness to it that I'd never noticed before. The sheep was eating grass peacefully and her little one was running around in circles, enjoying its mother's company. I could also hear birds chirping in the distance. If I could name the song that they were singing as they perched in the trees, I'd call it "Harmony". Time froze as I inhaled deeply and took in the moment. I was fully present and enjoying every bit of my existence. Soft breeze blew through the window and caressed my face. My feet were sitting snugly inside my extra fluffy bright yellow house slippers. My blue sarong wrap hung loosely on my body, keeping me cool and comfy. I felt a sense of calm, peace and a deep gratitude that filled my stomach. It almost felt like butterflies, but they were all still. I don't think I had ever experienced gratitude to that extent before. It felt surreal. Everything felt just right. I was thankful for all that I was, all that I had and all that I was experiencing in that very moment. Nothing else was on my mind. The feeling that that moment ignited was so deep and so intense, that I immediately went to my journal and wrote about it. It also set the mood for one my sweetest and most peaceful days.

If anyone ever asked me to describe what gratitude looks like, I'd tell that story. Nothing special at all happened that day. Nothing out of the ordinary. But gratitude appeared at my doorstep, and I let her in without hesitation. Without resistance. She thanked me for my hospitality that day by filling my home and my heart with so much love and so much peace. I wish a moment of gratitude like this on all of mankind.

Before that moment though, I had to work tirelessly on my relationship with gratitude. That wasn't the first time she showed up randomly. It was just the first time I deliberately let her in. I was first formally introduced to consciously and intentionally showing gratitude in therapy. I struggled with it. Terribly. After my therapist introduced gratitude as a practice, I did my own reading and research and I decided to set a challenge for myself. For 30 days, I'd write down three things I was grateful for daily. I was in a very low space at the time and I couldn't find much to put on my gratitude list. Almost every day, I was recycling the same things.

"I'm grateful for life."

"I'm grateful for a job."

"I'm grateful for family."

"I'm grateful for health."

"I'm grateful for food."

Then around day 20, I got really quiet and spent some time reflecting on my life. I saw the daily miracles and the "small things" that were an absolute gift – the people that loved me, checked on me and showed up for me, a safe space to live, the opportunity to create and to love and to express myself, the experiences that helped grow me, the opportunities that made me better, just to name a few. I dug even deeper. I was grateful for every meal that I was able to eat although I barely had an appetite. I expressed gratitude for every peaceful night's rest. I was grateful for every moment I had where I could laugh at a joke and feel a sense of ease. I had friends willing to listen to me and offer a comforting word – gratitude! I was still willing to help others and it made me feel better doing so – gratitude! I was able to function at work and make it through the day without crying – gratitude! Eventually the list was overflowing and since then, I've used gratitude as a tool to pull myself out of dark places and I'm now sharing this tool with you. For me, it's difficult to give thanks and really mean it when I'm feeling down, but it always gets easier over time and sets the tone for the days going forward. The times that it feels most difficult are likely when you need to open your mind and your heart to gratitude most.

Gratitude – Introduction to the Challenge

Life is a whirlwind, a rollercoaster ride, a seesaw, a crazy mixed bag of ups and downs and in-betweens. I can attest to the fact that it's not always easy to feel grateful, especially when in the middle of a storm. The same way that weeds don't need active care and maintenance to grow, low vibrational emotions don't need any efforts on your part to come to the surface and fester during difficult times. It's automatic. It's instinctual. You should acknowledge and accept these emotions and understand what they are trying to tell you. Make that your first priority. Feelings of sadness and worry during sickness, for example, mean that you care about your health and have a strong desire to recover from the illness. Feelings of anger when someone has done something that you don't like shows that they crossed a line; maybe betrayed your trust or disrespected one of your boundaries. Those are all natural emotional reactions. Just like happiness, excitement and pride are natural too, except that you don't like how the former ones feel. Don't let your discomfort with how an emotion moves through you be your reason to sidestep it. If you do this, it will just find another way to manifest itself. So, feel the emotion. Understand it. Whenever the time is right for you individually, let it go. In the midst of feeling a range of uncomfortable emotions, it is easy to let them overwhelm you and then you feel stuck. Gratitude can come into play here. But don't feel guilty if you and gratitude aren't really getting along right now. What I do want you to do, though, is open your mind to the idea of mending your relationship. It will benefit you in so many ways. I promise. Gratitude is a friend that comes to make your life easier and make the burdens feel just a little lighter so that you gather the strength to trod on a little further.

ACTIVITY: 5-Day Pre-Challenge – Gratitude Through the Senses

I'll start you off with the basics – giving thanks for your 5 senses. On each of the 5 days, complete the activity that will appeal to one of your 5 senses. Feel free to journal your thoughts as part of the activity for each day.

- Day 01 – Sight – Pick one of your favourite spots. It would be a plus if you're in nature. Nature is a natural recharger. The spot that you choose is entirely up to you. It could be the beach, a park, your backyard or even your favourite spot in the house. Sit quietly and look around. What is it that you like about this space? What catches your eye? Is anything different about the spot in this moment? What?

How does looking around and taking in the scenery make you feel? Can you envision your favourite memories in this spot?

- Day 02 – Sound – Choose a song. The genre doesn't matter. The song just has to be one that resonates with you and makes you feel good. Maybe the lyrics of the song bring you hope. Or joy. Or peace. Maybe it's just an instrumental and the drums in the beat awaken your heart and soul. The choice is yours. Play the song more than once. Close your eyes and really listen to the music. Let it completely absorb you. According to Alice Honig, PhD, professor emerita at Syracuse University who researches child development and human behaviour, "When you listen to a song over and over again, it can help you do some reflective listening to think, what are some of my feelings that this song is helping me get in tune with?" Ask yourself that question. Also, what do you like most about the song? Are there any lyrics that uplift you and help you through? What does hearing the song make you feel like doing? Is there any noticeable difference in how you felt before and after listening to the song a few times?

- Day 03 – Smell – Choose one of your favourite scents. Make sure that it's a scent you can easily get your hands on because you'll need to smell it as part of the exercise. It can be any kind of scent – a perfume, fresh laundry, a candle, incense, an air freshener, an essential oil, the scent of fresh bread in the oven, just to name a few. Create the scent in the air. Light that candle. Or bake that bread. Close your eyes and inhale deeply a few times. Really focus on that smell filling your nostrils. Is it a strong smell or a subtle one? What exactly do you like about it? Maybe it's comforting. Maybe you just like the hints of vanilla or cinnamon. How does it make you feel? Is it a feeling of peace, excitement, nostalgia? Does it bring back any memories? Maybe it reminds you of a summer's breeze or when you used to spend vacations with your grandmother.

- Day 04 – *Taste* – This one just might be everyone's favourite day. It's time to awaken those taste buds! Have you ever taken that first bite of a food that you were really looking forward to? And it was absolutely amazing, surpassing your expectations? You practically dribble as you begin to chew. You savour every moment between the first bite and the last swallow. That's the experience I want you to have with taste during this exercise, so choose the meal that you'd like to indulge in the most. Treat yourself to it! Or if you'd prefer, choose a drink that you really love – maybe a glass of red wine or a cup of coffee. Or it could be your favourite dessert – cake or ice cream, for example. Just choose something that you will thoroughly enjoy. When you have your drink or meal, try to be a present as possible. Eat or drink mindfully with no distractions. How did that first taste make you feel? Was it something sweet or savoury that you had? What was the taste like? What do you like most about this food/drink? How did you feel after you were all done in comparison to before?

- Day 05 – Touch – Think about something that feels warm and cozy to you. Is it the feeling of fresh sheets? Or fuzzy socks? Snuggling with your pet? A particular sweater you wear sometimes? Alternatively, choose an activity where you connect with yourself through touch. A long soak in the bathtub. A nice full body moisturize. A foot massage. A neck massage. You choose. As long as you feel comforted through touch while carrying out the activity. Once again, be fully present. Describe what it feels like as best as you can. What do you like about the sensation? Is it something soft to the touch on your hand or skin? What thoughts come up in your mind? How does it make you feel? Detail the emotions that you experience.

You can complete this exercise as many times as you like, choosing different stimuli each time. Most importantly, tune into how each of your senses can increase the joy and gratitude that you get out of each activity.

ACTIVITY: 21-Day Challenge – Gratitude Through Reflection

This challenge aims to help you reflect on the great things that have happened to you so far in your journey, that have contributed positively to who you are now. Maybe life feels extremely challenging in this moment. But in the grand scheme of things, you're more blessed than you realize. I hope that you discover something beautiful during this 21-day challenge. Happy journaling!

Day 01 – Write down the name of someone that helped you in your younger days. Call or message them and tell them thank you if they're still alive to receive their flowers. If they have passed, write a letter addressed to them.

Day 02 – Write about 1 thing that you learned that positively shaped your perspective on life.

Day 03 – Write about a challenge that you overcame and the lesson that you walked away with.

Day 04 – Write about an activity you enjoyed as a child. Do it today, or before the end of the challenge, if possible!

Day 05 – Write about your greatest accomplishment in life thus far.

Day 06 – Write down the name of a movie or video that inspired you in the past. Rewatch it if you can!

Day 07 – Write about something that you created that you're proud of. Take a look at it if possible.

Day 08 – Write about a happy memory that comforts you.

Day 09 – Write about a gift that you received that still helps you in some way today.

Day 10 – Write down a quote that has always motivated or inspired you. Change the background on your computer, tablet or phone to this quote so that you can see it every day until the end of this challenge.

Day 11 – Write about something that made you laugh recently.

Day 12 – Write about one way that you have grown in the past year.

Day 13 – Write about your favourite vacation to date.

Day 14 – Write about something in nature that always lifts your spirits. Do it today, or before the end of the challenge, if possible.

Day 15 – Write about a compliment that you received that made you feel better about yourself.

Day 16 – Write about a friendship you value and why. Share what you've written with that friend.

Day 17 – Write about your favourite memory with a family member. Call or message them and share that memory and a "thank you" today. If they have passed, write a letter addressed to them.

Day 18 – Write about an activity that makes you feel at ease and carefree. Do it today, or before the end of the challenge, if possible.

Day 19 – Write about a place you visited where you thoroughly enjoyed the experience and customer service. It could be a bar, a restaurant, a movie theatre, etc. Leave a review on their social media page or website, if possible.

Day 20 – Write down what you love about yourself (at least 5 qualities/attributes/physical features). Read it out loud! Soak in the love and gratitude for self!

Day 21 – Write about why you're grateful for this challenge and any beautiful things you discovered over the 21 days.

Why Is Gratitude Important?

As you're reading through the gratitude exercises, you might be wondering why gratitude is so important. Showing gratitude can literally make you feel happier and improve your overall well-being. By intentionally focusing on the things you're grateful for, you're bringing other emotions like joy, pleasure and peace to the forefront. It can also help to shape your perspective, giving you a more positive outlook on whatever challenges you face, and on life itself. Sometimes, it's tempting to mumble and grumble non-stop when you feel as though a dark cloud is constantly over you, following you no matter where you turn. But when you see and acknowledge that silver lining – gratitude, suddenly the cloud isn't so grey anymore. And over time, the sun starts to peep out.

There has even been extensive research on the effects of gratitude on an individual's well-being. One study in particular stood out to me. According to the Harvard Health Publishing website, harvard.edu, two psychologists, Dr. Robert A. Emmons and Dr.

Michael E. McCullough carried out a study where they asked participants to write a few sentences each week, focusing on particular topics that the psychologists provided. One group wrote about things that occurred that they were grateful for, another wrote about things that had upset or irritated them, while the third group wrote about events that had affected them, with no emphasis on them being positive or negative. When the study concluded 10 weeks later, those who wrote about gratitude were more optimistic and felt better about their lives. They also exercised more and had fewer visits to physicians than their counterparts. This was a simple study and the results spoke volumes. Gratitude has a positive impact on mental health, which in turn affects your daily choices and the way that you live.

As you delve deeper into your gratitude practice, I want you to remember that gratitude is more than words. It's more than saying "I'm grateful." Gratitude is something that you feel deeply so it manifests in your actions and habits. If you're complaining constantly about all the things that are going wrong, even though you wrote in your gratitude journal earlier that morning, chances are you're not truly embracing gratitude as a practice. Instead, take a step back when things feel overwhelming. Focus on your circle of control. This is always important. Now, think about the things going in your favour. Everything can't be all wrong. It's okay if you still feel overwhelmed, frustrated, sad or any other difficult emotion.

Life is about duality. You can be grateful and also overwhelmed. You can be thankful and also tired. The power is within you to decide which emotion you're going to feed. You decide when you want to shift your focus and what you'll shift it to. As long as you go through the process with patience and self-compassion, you're doing it right! Remember, it took me a long time to open the door to gratitude. But I didn't stop trying. There will be times of total frustration and feeling like you're not getting anywhere. There will also be times that you take a break – maybe a short one, or a long one. This is why patience and self-compassion need to accompany you along the way.

As you lean into gratitude, it's also important to note that gratitude is not complacency. Don't feel guilty for wanting things to change. Don't feel guilty for wanting a situation to improve. Don't feel guilty for wanting to grow and transform. Don't feel guilty for wanting more. You deserve more. Remember the duality of life that I mentioned? Here it is again. Remember the talk about acceptance before working on change? Here it is again too. You can express genuine gratitude for this particular stage in life and also see it for what it is – a steppingstone. It's a temporary situation in the journey. If you feel grateful that you have a job and you're able to afford certain luxuries, but you're still applying for other jobs because you know that you can and want to do more, that's fine.

Both feelings can exist simultaneously. That's what growth is all about.

QUICK TIP: Gratitude in Manifestation

Manifestation is a very in-depth and intricate process. Although this book won't go into detail about how to manifest the things you want, below is some information about the role that gratitude plays in the process.

Gratitude in Manifestation - What Is Manifestation?

Manifestation is the act of bringing the things that you focus on to your physical reality through thoughts, attraction, feelings and beliefs. We can manifest both good and bad things, and we can do so either consciously or unconsciously. You might be manifesting without even noticing the part that you played through your thoughts and actions. Think about that thing that you would really like – a promotion, a partner, a family, a change in career, your own business. You're trying your best to get it. Or at least you think so. You're praying about it. But do you really think that you deserve it? Or is there a tiny voice inside telling you that you can't get it, or that it won't happen? Consciously, and logically, you're telling yourself it's possible and you're working towards it. But that seemingly tiny subconscious voice is actually a loud scream scaring away your manifestations – stopping them from making it to reality. The subconscious is creating a block so you're not able to consciously manifest what you desire. You have to work through that blockage and limiting belief to get the wheels spinning on your manifestation process.

Gratitude in Manifestation – How Are They Connected?

As you know by now, gratitude is so powerful that it can shift your entire mindset and put you in a more positive space mentally. It creates a state of abundance within you. Gratitude is like the fertilizer for your goals and dreams. On the other hand, limiting beliefs and ungratefulness can be seen as poison, slowly eating away at your goals and dreams until nothing is left. That is, if you don't intervene. You can't consciously manifest your desires if your mind is constantly flooded with ungrateful thoughts. You must work through those emotions and come to a calm space, where fruitful and peaceful thoughts can bloom. Gratitude can actually help you come to this space. It's all about what you focus on. Work through the bad, so that you can focus on the good that you already have. Once you shift your energy to a positive frequency, you attract like energy. It's that simple. Positive thoughts bring positive experiences.

You can go a step further with your gratitude practice. Ever thought about showing gratitude for the things that you desire, as if they were there already? Feel and speak your dreams into existence. Remember the voice that tells you it's not possible? It's time to quiet that voice. Close your eyes and envision yourself with the things that you want. Really feel it. What are your emotions after manifesting the things that you want? What are your thoughts? Feel everything as if it were your current reality. Don't hold back. This exercise puts you in the emotional state of already having what you want. Eventually, your mind becomes accustomed to these emotions and thus, it lets go of the subconscious thought patterns of unworthiness.

Once you strengthen your gratitude practice, let it join hands with your manifestation practice and watch the reality that you desire unfold right before your eyes. And as beautiful and extraordinary as it will be, you won't be surprised because you know it's exactly what was meant for you and you worked so hard for it.

Love

Love - An intense feeling of deep affection *(Lexico Online Dictionary)*

Self-Love - Regard for one's own well-being and happiness (chiefly considered as a desirable rather than narcissistic characteristic) *(Lexico Online Dictionary)*

Self-Love *(for the context of this book)* – The positive feelings that you have for yourself and the way that these feelings allow you to show up for and take care of yourself *(Shakira Stuart)*

I let go

I let go of their expectations

I let go of their rules and regulations

I let go

I let go of my fears

I let go of my doubts and despair

I let go

I let go of who they bullied me to be

I let go of what they'd think of me

I let go

I let go of holding in my truth

I let go of unspoken words that kept me subdued

I let go

I let go of putting myself last

I let go of doing whatever I was asked

I let go

I let go

I let go

Cornered with my back against the wall

I had no choice but to release

I finally said "I choose me"

And those very words

When they escaped my lips

Unshackled my ankles and my wrists

I was now free

I was now free to explore the unfiltered version of me

I was now free from mental and emotional slavery

I was now free

I was now free to lick my wounds

I was now free to plant myself anew, to bloom

I was now free

I was now free be the light

I was now free from worry that I was too bright

I was now free

I was now free to grow and explore

I was now free to see who I am at my core

I was now free

I was now free to take off my disguise

I was now free to love me without compromise

I was now free

I was now free

I was now free

- Black Tea & Honey

What Is Love to You?

Before we delve into the seed of love. I want you to take some time and reflect on the meaning of love for you. What does it look like? How has it shown up in your life? Has it helped you in any way? How? Do you think that it's important? Why?

You can choose to answer each of these questions. Or you can do a drawing/painting of what love looks like to you. Get as creative as you'd like and have fun with it!

What Is Love to Me?

Love has perhaps been one of the most impactful seeds of my personal self-transformation. Love, for me, was like the glue that held everything together. I'd go as far as to say that love was my super-seed. I say this because I had to learn to fall deeply in love with myself in order to practice **awareness** and **acceptance** in a healthy and meaningful way. Self-love usually talked me off the edge and took the self-loathing gun away when I felt overwhelmed during these practices. It wasn't always pretty! Love then held me gently and soothed me as I practiced **gratitude**. And just when I thought that love did all that it could do, love taught me to have **faith** in myself, to have **patience** with myself every step of the way, even when I made mistakes. And the culmination of my acts of love for myself was holding space for the person I am now while simultaneously practicing **discipline** and putting in the work to give myself everything that I desire and deserve.

Love didn't always look this way for me though. If you asked me what it looked like a few years ago, I'd paint a totally different picture. Back then, love meant romance. Love meant passion. Love meant sex. Love meant relationships. Love meant choosing hell with someone over peace in solitude. Love meant breaking up to make up. Love meant amazing highs and equally intense lows. Love was an adrenaline rush. Love was everything I saw in romance novels and movies. Love was flowers, kisses in the rain, soft giggles under the sheets, cute photos, date nights, and eventually kids and a "happy" family.

My idea of love manifested into my reality. I chased relationships and all the things that I thought love should be within those relationships. A lot of the time, I wasn't even in love with my partner. I was in love with my idea of love. And I was willing to do anything to make it work. Life has a funny way of teaching you lessons though. I had to learn some hard ones to change my idea of what love looks like. At one point, I even thought I was a love-addict. When I began therapy, I told my therapist this. I eventually figured out that I couldn't be addicted to something I never truly experienced. A lot of us try to give and receive love as best as we know how – whether in romantic, platonic or familial relationships

– but many times, the transfer of love is blocked by suffering, pain, trauma and toxic cycles. The first time I felt genuine, pure, undiluted love moving inside of me, I had given it to myself. I allowed myself to be vulnerable and let go of every subconscious belief about me being unlovable or difficult to love. I let go of thought patterns shaped by past experiences that scarred me and made me question my worth. I looked at myself as I was and decided that I deserved love. Yes, that version of me then and any other version too. I shouldn't have to work for it nor reach certain milestones to earn it. Love is my birthright. Love is your birthright. Love is our birthright. By just existing, by just being, by just breathing, we all deserve to be loved.

ACTIVITY: Mirror Work for Self-Love

We all feel unlovable from time to time. Maybe, you're holding onto deep shame, regret or self-loathing because of something that you did or went through. Maybe, you can't pinpoint the reason but sometimes you just don't feel worthy. This is the best time to practice speaking to yourself lovingly.

Have you ever heard of mirror work? It's a new-age practice where you meet your reflection in the mirror and send yourself loving messages and/or affirmations. Like the mirror exercise in an earlier chapter, this may feel a bit weird and out of your element at first.

That's okay. Great things happen outside of comfort zones, so still give it a try. If this makes it any easier, pretend that you're speaking to a friend that really needs loving reassurance right now. Maybe their life depends on it. What would you say to them? It's okay if you get emotional when you tell yourself the things you know that you need to hear. It's okay if you resist these words of affirmation at first – repeat them! Get comfortable with speaking to yourself in a loving and meaningful way. Say whatever you want to say – as long as it's loving. Be open and vulnerable with yourself. *Don't hold back during this practice.*

Below is a synopsis of what I've said to myself during a mirror work session:

I am mindful of the fact that love is my birthright. Love doesn't have to be a fight or a chase. Love flows freely to and from me. I am worthy of healthy love. I deserve loving and supportive friends and family. I deserve a loving and supportive partner too. I enforce my boundaries in all my relationships as an act of love for myself. I speak my truth unapologetically. It is okay to speak my truth even when my voice shakes because I deserve to be heard. The right persons will appreciate and embrace my honesty. I don't have to operate out of past trauma because I am healed, loved and supported. I am also worthy. I am here to be loved and cherished. I am patient with myself throughout these processes. Even when I make mistakes, I remember that I still deserve love, compassion and kindness. Even when I feel like the world isn't giving it to me, I give it to myself.

You can try saying these words to yourself if they resonate with you. Or you can write your own script. You can also choose to wing it and just let it flow, saying whatever comes to your mind in the moment. The choice is yours.

Love Is Healing

All of us have healing to do. All of us have been hurt at some point. Some of us address the pain. Others bury it. But the fact remains, we all experience some kind of pain. Just like we need to recover from physical injury, the same goes for mental and emotional injury. The treatment depends on the severity of the injury. If you fall and hurt your leg, causing it to become swollen and painful, I am sure that you will automatically think of a plan of action to relieve the pain. You might get some ice for the swelling and rest so that you don't put unnecessary pressure on the leg. You might even go to the doctor to have it checked out. You should take a similar approach when you're experiencing emotional turmoil. For example, after a bad breakup, take time to offer yourself love and compassion as you grieve the ending of the relationship. Explore activities that can lift your spirit. Talk to a friend or a therapist if you feel like you can't process the pain alone. Every action that you take during your emotional pain should be an act of love for yourself and your healing.

Love literally heals you. According to experts, experiencing the feeling of love causes your body to release endorphins which relieve stress and pain. The level of the stress hormone – cortisol – is simultaneously reduced. Issues such as anxiety, high blood pressure and depression can also be reduced through experiencing the feeling of love. Although the results of these studies were based heavily on love in relationships with others, the healing power of self-love shouldn't be overlooked. By exploring self-love, you become more aware of how to nurture and take care of yourself. Self-love looks like speaking to yourself positively, eating well, getting enough rest, walking away from people and situations that drain you, amongst other things. Self-love also sets the tone for the relationships with others in your life.

Committing to acts of love for yourself and even for others can work wonders for your healing journey. The times that I felt most down and out, I realized that I got a deep and profound joy from donating to or assisting a charity. Knowing that I could lift someone's spirit and be of service, in turn, lifted mine. Of course, I was also committing to acts of love for myself. As the adage saying goes, you can't pour from an empty cup. I was journaling, writing poetry, reading spiritual material and reciting my affirmations. I was letting love flow through me as I tended to my wounds. These acts caused me to naturally gravitate towards charity as part of my healing. I never felt forced nor pressured. Whenever I do charity work, it is always a genuine desire to share love and healing. Everything is energy. And healing energy is especially powerful. Just like I did, research and explore various methods for your healing. You will find what resonates with you. Each of us is different so I won't give one recipe for healing through love. It's up to you to create your own personal recipe.

ACTIVITY: Heal Your Body, Mind & Spirit – Weekly Challenge

Each week commit to one activity to heal your body, mind and spirit. Make a special effort to commit for 8 weeks!

Before you begin the challenge, journal about how you feel about your healing journey right now. Do you think there is any healing that you need to do? Have you ever consciously healed from anything?

Jump into the challenge whenever you feel like the time is right! Mix up your activities as much as you'd like. Or you can choose one activity from each group and practice it once every week. Get an accountability buddy for extra encouragement if you think you might need it. Keep it fun and engaging.

Activities for healing the body can look like:

Preparing a healthy meal

Exercising

Walking

Practicing yoga

Swimming

Dancing

Moving meditation

Activities for healing the mind can look like:

Meditating

Reading books for personal development

Listening to podcasts for personal development

Eating mindfully

Practicing breathwork exercises

Fixing a puzzle

Listening to uplifting music with a positive message

Activities for healing the spirit can look like:

Praying

Spending time alone in nature

Journaling

Serving others/charity work

Practicing deep reflection

Meditating

Love Is Nurturing

Imagine the relationship between a mother and her child. Imagine the love that she has for her offspring and the way that she expresses it. She makes her child feel seen, heard, supported and appreciated. She offers words of encouragement. She offers guidance. She offers comfort. All of this is done in an effort to see her child not only grow and develop as they should, but also thrive.

Growth and development don't suddenly stop in adulthood. It just looks different. We're no longer learning to crawl, walk and identify letters and numbers. Most of our physical development has also ended. Now, there's a heavy focus on personal and career development. We learn more about ourselves, our characters, our personalities and we have goals, dreams and aspirations. We can't reach these goals without a certain level of growth and development. The bigger your goals, the more work you'll have to do on yourself. It's often a difficult process.

Then why do we forget to nurture ourselves through this process? The same nurturing that a mother should give to her child is what you need to give to yourself if you want to excel. Mommy is no longer responsible for you in that way and you're no longer dependent. Now, you have to take the reins and nurture yourself, your own inner child, as you continue to grow into the person that you envision.

We all have an inner child. We are every age we've ever been. Those experiences in our younger years help shape many of our conscious and unconscious beliefs. Some of our biggest insecurities and wounds were birthed during our childhood and can manifest in different ways in adulthood. Let's say you were constantly teased by your older sibling for crying whenever you felt sad. They called you a big baby and made fun of you until you were absolutely inconsolable. "Boys don't cry. Only sissies do." You heard this every time you cried. Even if you just shed one tear. Eventually, you learned how to ignore your sadness so that you don't end up crying. You learned how to completely bottle up your emotions. This tactic walks all the way to adulthood with you. You become indifferent and don't know how to express yourself when a situation makes you sad or emotional. Instead of facing the emotion, you shut down. You also avoid emotionally charged conversations and situations. This impacts your romantic relationships negatively. More importantly, it impacts your relationship with yourself. You're not holding space for yourself to process difficult emotions. Your inner child continues to feel stifled and silenced. Only through acknowledgement and nurturing of your traumatized inner child, can you heal this wound lovingly.

This is an issue that many men face - that inability to safely and healthily express their emotions because they were conditioned not to. Whether the pressures came from a sibling, a parent, school peers or society, there's this distorted image being painted of what a man should look like. Expression of sadness is often traded in for open displays of anger and aggression or indifference. This is viewed as more acceptable.

This isn't limited to men only. Growing up, I myself was often told that I was too emotional. One time my grandmother even threatened that if I kept crying so much, I could cause myself to get a heart attack. At such a tender age, I believed her without question. I eventually adopted the thought pattern that I was too emotional. I apologized for crying. I apologized for getting worked up. I bottled up my emotions until I had outbursts of sadness and uncontrollable crying. Only when I consoled my inner child and let her know that it is okay to feel and to cry, was I better able to express my emotions without having those uncontrollable outbursts on people. I allow myself to feel every single emotion and take my time working through them. I nurture myself throughout the process without judgement. I remind myself that "too emotional" is relative. The right persons will hold space for my big emotions. I set an example by holding space for them myself whenever they arise. I now stand behind this practice for working through big emotions.

ACTIVITY: Dear Younger Me - A Letter To Your Inner Child

Reflect on your childhood for a few minutes. Think of a time that you needed nurturing love the most and did not receive it. Maybe it was when you failed a big exam and felt ashamed and disappointed in yourself. Maybe it was when your parents divorced and left you feeling sad and broken. Maybe it was when you entered adolescence and felt insecure due to bullying and taunting by your peers. There isn't a reason that's too small or too big. Whatever reason you had for feeling the way you did, is valid. Write a letter to the most vulnerable part of your inner child and make them feel seen, heard, supported and appreciated.

Love Is Unconditional

Above all else, love is unconditional. If it is not unconditional, then it is not love. Let's start with you and the love you have for yourself. Regardless of what your past or present look like – things that you're ashamed of, wrongs that you committed, mistreatment from others that you endured, self-destructive behaviour that you engaged in, times that you knew better but didn't do better – no matter the circumstance or what you are currently doing or did previously, you deserve to love yourself unconditionally. Yes, you read that right. You deserve to love yourself unconditionally. Say it aloud *"I deserve to love myself unconditionally. I commit to loving myself unconditionally from this moment forward."*

Unconditional love doesn't mean that you avoid your mistakes, pretend that you're perfect or that you won't face consequences for your actions. Unconditional love means that you love yourself despite mistakes, imperfection, consequences, trauma, pain and suffering. You still hold yourself accountable. You still try to do better. You just remember that love for yourself is priority no matter what. Furthermore, the times that you feel your lowest and that you're doing your worst, love yourself even more fiercely. Be intentional and assertive with your self-love. This is the time you're likely to beat yourself up the most and engage in negative self-talk. It's time to rewrite the script by trading in this habit for a more uplifting one. Remind yourself that you are loved by you unconditionally and that matters most. It's okay to say "I made a mistake. I feel badly about it. I offer myself unconditional love as I work through this feeling because I want to do and be better going forward." Let the unconditional love for yourself assist you as you work through your emotions. Judgmental self-talk like "I'm so stupid to have done that. How foolish could I be?" is unhelpful at best and extremely destructive at worst. Accept that you made a mistake or did something wrong. Own up to it but don't become it. If you practice this often enough, those self-talks rooted in the unconditional love that you have for yourself, can even help you to avoid certain mistakes or self-destructive behaviours going forward. You'll become more intentional about doing what's best for you and more committed to acts of self-love and self-preservation.

Let's say you're an alcoholic and this is your fifth time trying to quit the habit. After a long time reminding yourself that you deserve unconditional self-love, you might tell yourself "I promised that I'd work on my drinking problem and beat the habit this time, but I'm tempted to drink right now because of how sad I feel. I know that I will feel worse in the morning if I get drunk tonight. The guilt and shame will consume me, and it will be hard to pull myself out of that space. I love myself unconditionally so I will do my best to avoid putting myself through that again. My friend told me that anytime I feel the urge to drink, I can call her, and we can do something to help me through the night. I'll call her now because I want to do better." Sometimes, having that rational conversation with yourself beforehand, and reminding yourself that you're loved unconditionally and want to be better, can guide you to make better decisions. Show yourself unconditional love and move in unconditional love.

Loving yourself unconditionally also opens space for you to love others unconditionally. You might ask yourself why this is even necessary. Well, unconditional love is the foundation for creating healthy relationships with others. You should care for those in your life and want the best for them, even if it doesn't benefit you. Very often our love for others is based on their role in our life, our attachment to each other and it sometimes becomes possessive. When I was much younger, I remember telling a boyfriend that I loved him so much and wanted us to stay together no matter what. He promised that we would. I also told him that I wouldn't want to see him with anyone else if we ever broke up. I swore that I loved him unconditionally. But did I really love him unconditionally if I was hoping that he wouldn't find love again just to spare my feelings? Did I really love him unconditionally if I wanted him with me or no one else? Unconditional love is wishing him the best if we grow apart. It's hoping that he finds the love for him and I find the one for me, if we realize that we are no longer compatible. Unconditional love is praying that he finds healing if his own suffering caused him to hurt me. Unconditional love is letting him go if the relationship becomes destructive or abusive to me. That's unconditional love! And really, if we practiced unconditional love more, we'd lovingly part ways with persons when they are no longer supposed to journey with us. If someone disrespected your boundaries and although you've addressed it with them, they persist, unconditional love allows you to wish them the best and step away from the relationship. This is a strong act of love for both you and the person hurting you. Only someone else that understands and moves in unconditional love would see this for what it is. Unconditional love doesn't want to own you, expect anything from you nor attach to you. Unconditional love holds space for you and wants the best for you. There's a saying that summarizes this beautifully. *"When you like a flower, you just pluck it. But when you love a flower, you water it daily."*

ACTIVITY: Trade in The Bat for The Blue Ribbon

Since we are practicing self-talks rooted in unconditional love, this is the perfect exercise.

We've all beat ourselves up for a mistake, a behaviour, a characteristic or a physical trait we'd like to change. One hundred percent of the time this only makes us feel worse. I've never heard anyone say, "I feel so much better today after spending the entire night angry and scolding myself for the mistake I made." Have you? I bet not!

So, it's time to be gentle with yourself. Follow the steps below.

1. Stop beating yourself up.
2. Put the bat down.
3. Pick up the blue ribbon.
4. Pin it to your chest and acknowledge the winner in you!

What are 3 things that you beat yourself up for? What are some positive thoughts that you can counteract these defeating thoughts with? Show yourself some unconditional love as you work through this one.

Here's an example: "I usually beat myself up for getting distracted too easily. Right now, I choose to instead commend myself for making efforts to get back on track after each distraction."

What A Lack of Self-Love Looks Like

Now that you've delved into showing love for yourself and others, I think that it's also important to highlight what a lack of self-love looks like. So many of us are lacking self-love and don't even see it. It usually manifests in two major ways — allowing mistreatment from others and mistreating others.

Most of us know a person that claims they are too kind, and they're always being taken advantage of. They stay in draining, toxic and sometimes abusive relationships. They allow persons to hurt them over and over and never walk away. I know this type of person oh too well because it was once me and I am not afraid to say it. In my healing journey, I realized that I attracted and clung to the type of persons I thought I deserved. What I accepted directly reflected my level of self-love and self-worth. Deep inside I always thought I could do no better and being mistreated felt like a better option than feeling lonely. Going inward and facing myself was one of the toughest and most liberating things I've ever done in my life. If you're allowing others to treat you poorly and you keep forgiving them, ask yourself "Do I really love myself unconditionally and do my actions reflect such?"

Most of us also know a person who is mean, destructive and maybe even abusive. Maybe they mistreat everyone or maybe they just mistreat those closest to them, like their lover or their parents. So many times, this is a silent cry for help. This person also feels unworthy and lacks self-love. They fear allowing someone to truly love them and to embrace that love because they think that they don't deserve it. There's a lot of unspoken pain and anger in a person like this. I've seen it so many times because this is the type that I often attracted. It's no surprise that persons who allow themselves to be mistreated, attract those that constantly mistreat others. There's a lesson that they need to learn from each other. When each of them will learn it is the question that I don't have an answer to. I went through similar situations over and over, one after the next, until it completely broke me down and then I saw the light. Hopefully, this can save at least one person from hitting their version of rock bottom. The sooner you see the light, the sooner you can begin your healing. If you find yourself lashing out at others, getting extremely angry, being emotionally or physically abusive, ask yourself "Do I really love myself unconditionally and do my actions reflect such?"

Faith

Faith - Confidence or trust in a person or thing *(Dictionary.com)*

Faith *(for the context of this book)* – Deep belief and trust in someone or something without the need for tangible/physical proof of its existence and/or power *(Shakira Stuart)*

I am...

My ancestors' wildest dream

I am

The one to break the curse

Of suffering

Of defeat

Of poverty

I am

The one to close the door

Take a detour

Walk roads foreign to my bleeding feet

To escort my bloodline to victory

I am

The one to gather riches

And when I say riches

I don't just mean possessions

I'm speaking on something

Way more important

Rich soul

Rich spirit

Rich life

Rich vibe

I am

The one to bring us all alive

We'll no longer have to just cope

And fail every time that we try

I am

The one that you'll call the sacrifice

I'll put my blood, sweat and tears

Into getting us where

We all deserve to be

We all deserve a seat

We all deserve to eat

I am

The one to bring the table

The food

The water

The fruit of the earth

And the dessert

I am

The one to prepare the feast

I'll say the prayer

Before we eat

Bless every mouth that I feed

Bless every crop that I reap

In order to prepare the table before me

I am

The one to end mental slavery

We may not be in chains

But I feel the whips and lashes

Raining down on our brains

A system built to see us barely get by

To take what little we have and hope we die

Before we can claim it back

And to disguise it as fair

They call it tax

I am

The one to get down on my hands and knees

Get my skin dusty and fingers bloody

To return us to royalty

Make sure we are crowned

And burn this whole system

Right down

To the very ground

That we deserve to walk on

Without having to pay a fee

I am

Part of something

Much bigger than me

I am

The change

I am

History

His story

Her story

I am

Everything they said

We could not be

And while I work

To destroy

And rebuild

Unlearn

And learn

Give back

And earn

I ask that you

Just have faith in me

- Black Tea & Honey

Laying the Foundation for Faith

I asked you to first be aware of yourself. Consciously aware. Deliberately aware. I asked that you delve into parts of yourself that you previously didn't notice. Then I asked you to accept the things you became aware of. The good. The bad. The ugly. All of it. No matter how you perceive it. Then I went a step further and asked you to show gratitude for who you are and all that you have. Give thanks for your very existence. To be here. To be breathing. To be reading these words. Give thanks for all of it. You might want to change some things, but you've come so far already. You've learned so much and grown so much. I asked that you be grateful each step of the way along your journey. Then I took a big leap and asked you to develop a deep healing, nurturing and unconditional love for yourself. No matter the circumstance. A love that speaks positively to you. A love that uplifts you. A love that makes you want to do better. A love that makes you better. All those steps were deliberately placed one after the other, in order to get you to this one. Faith. I want you to have an unshakable faith in yourself and your abilities. You'll need this faith if you want to maximize your true potential. If you cannot believe it, you cannot manifest it. It's really that simple.

I've asked you to wake up and go deep within. With every page I was taking you further inward. I was laying the foundation for faith. I want you to know and love yourself so strongly that nothing can

116

make you stop believing in you. Life isn't easy. It was never meant to be. It will test you over and over. What makes it even more complicated is that there's no instruction manual. Of course, you get a few pointers here and there. A bunch of life lessons through firsthand experience. Maybe some advice from someone who experienced a similar situation to yours. But a step-by-step guide? Nope! There's no crystal ball telling you exactly what your future will be like – the journey, the path to take, the detours you'll have to make. I'm sure that so many things happened to you in life, sometimes completely devastating, sometimes unimaginably wonderful. What they both had in common is that you never saw them coming. The surprise usually makes the event even more impactful. Life's unpredictability is also part of its beauty. A quiet, sometimes dark, unassuming beauty. When you move in faith, you lean into this unpredictability with a childlike curiosity and amazement. This in turn allows you to get so much more out of life, as you deserve.

Don't be intimidated because life is unpredictable. Don't be intimidated because you can't control some outcomes. This is your first time having this human experience. But it doesn't mean that you have to turn on autopilot and just let life happen to you. Dare to envision your biggest dreams. Dare to think about something you really want. Dare to believe that it can happen. Dare to go after it. Dare to move in faith!

ACTIVITY: S P E L L   O U T   Y O U R   G O A L S

Those goals that you have? As long as you're willing to put in the work, you can achieve them. You have what it takes. So, act like you do. It's time to stop ignoring the dreamer in you. Instead, encourage it. Neo soul singer Erykah Badu once tweeted *"Write it down on real paper with a real pencil with real intent and watch it get real. Spelling is a Spell."*

I want you to remember that! Writing down your goals helps you to create a clearer vision in your mind of what you want to achieve. After all, you won't start to build a house without having the blueprints. You want to be able to see what it should look like in order to bring the idea to life. Think of your goals this way too. Write it down, think about it and imagine yourself doing it. This is a simple way to build your faith in yourself and your abilities when it comes to achieving those goals that you have. Faith is an integral part of execution.

Get your journal and answer the following questions:

- What are your goals for the next week?
- What are your goals for the rest of this year?
- What can you do differently to come closer to achieving them?

I'll go ahead and share mine with you. Just to drive my point home, by the time you're reading this, these goals would have already been achieved.

- *My goals for the next week are to finish this chapter on Faith and also finish part 1 of the book I am currently reading called "The Joy of Living" by Yongey Mingyur Rinpoche & Eric Swanson.*
- *My major goals for the rest of the year are to finish writing my book and find an editor and publisher to work with.*
- *I'm committed to reducing my social media time and instead, set aside more time for writing. I've previously spent a lot of time consumed by distractions and I want to change that.*

What Does F.A.I.T.H. Entail?

Whenever you're feeling down and discouraged, remember that each letter in the word faith has a powerful meaning. Let it serve as your reminder to keep believing in yourself and keep pushing on no matter what. Also, let it serve as your guide to what to do to keep your faith strong.

F – Filter out your fear

A – Affirm yourself

I – Imagine the best possible outcome

T – Trust that if it is for you, it will happen

H – Have Patience

Filter Out Your Fear

Bob Proctor, Canadian self-help author and philosopher, once said "Faith and fear have a lot in common, they both demand you believe in something you cannot see. You choose!" Most of the time, we have so many trivial fears that stand in the way of us truly going after our dreams. Fear of failure. Fear of rejection. Fear of looking silly. Fear of starting over. Fear of doing it alone. Sometimes this fear is based on previous experiences that left a sour taste in our mouths. Other times, this fear is just a manifestation of us dwelling on the worst possible outcome in order to discourage ourselves from making another step forward. Regardless of the origin, fear is just another natural human emotion. One that you are quite capable of working through. When it comes to you, your potential and your abilities, see fear as a foreign substance that needs to be filtered out of your system. Do you know what you'll be using to get this fear out? A whole lot of faith! You can't have strong fear and strong faith at the same time. Like Bob Proctor said, choose which one you want to work with. The answer should be a no brainer. But in case you need a further nudge in the right direction, think about which one is most likely to propel you forward, to make you do more, to help you achieve those goals. Now, let go of the one that doesn't serve you. This takes us to the "A" in F.A.I.T.H.

Affirm Yourself

To really filter out that fear, you need to replace those fearful thoughts with faithful ones. Trade in the self-limiting belief for one that works in your favour. We did affirmation exercises before, so this is already familiar. Let's say that you have a fear of public speaking. You want to do a presentation to pitch an idea to a charity, but fear keeps intervening. Fear is saying, "You don't know enough to pitch that idea. They'll laugh in your face. You'll embarrass yourself. They won't even let you finish the presentation if you even get a chance to do it." It makes no sense trying to filter out these fears without some strategy. Just telling yourself "forget those negative thoughts" is like trying to filter mud out of water by using your fingers to take out the bits and grains. It will take you forever and you'll never be able to remove all of the impurities that way. Instead, a water filtration system would work wonders. Your affirmations rooted in faith in yourself take the job as the filtration system. So, before you call to make your appointment to do the presentation and every time fear creeps in before the presentation, remind yourself "I am smart and knowledgeable about the topic I am presenting on. I have prepared well. My ideas need to be heard. I welcome respectful and constructive criticism on my presentation. I see it as an opportunity to gain more knowledge, in addition to sharing my knowledge." You keep reminding yourself that you deserve this opportunity and you will take it because you deserve to take it. You affirm yourself as many times as you need to, even if you have to take a short moment and do it silently during your presentation. Face your fear and filter it out. Then you'll have so much more room for faith to expand.

Imagine the Best Possible Outcome

If you're thinking about possibilities, think about all of them. Why only consider the worst-case scenario? Give some energy to the best-case ones too. And any other scenarios in between. This can be especially helpful when it comes to planning. You might foresee possible obstacles and create strategies for overcoming them, or at least an idea of how you'll face them. I think it's worth it to write down all the possible outcomes of a situation when your fear becomes especially debilitating. After you've gone through your scenarios and planned accordingly, then focus on the best possible outcome. After all, that's the outcome that you really want to bring to fruition. We underestimate the power and force of energy. If you're using your energy to focus on the worst outcomes, it's likely that this will lead you to feel discouraged and you may not put in your best effort. Even worse, you may not put in any effort at all because you won't see the point in trying if you're fixated on the possibility of this unfavourable outcome. Alternatively, devoting more time to focusing on the best possible outcome will allow you to maximize your efforts within your circle of control. The best possible outcome becomes the ribbon at the end of the race. That ribbon is no longer just a piece of material. It represents your determination and seeing the race through to the end. Visualization of the best possible outcome can be a source of motivation. Believing that you have the power to achieve it can boost your confidence which impacts your overall approach and efforts. It's that simple.

Trust That If It's for You, It Will Happen

This is where it gets tricky. Sometimes we tend to go from one extreme to the next. From feeling completely demotivated to obsessing over goals in an unhealthy way. From doing way too little to exhausting ourselves and doing way too much. This is where balance is important. It's okay to plan to achieve the best possible outcome while simultaneously being willing to accept other outcomes. Sometimes, we think we are sure that we want something and only when we don't receive it, then we realize that we were overlooking something else that becomes way more important. I remember when I really wanted to grow within a company that I was working at. I started out truly ambitious and putting in maximum effort. Over time, I realized that the company was not an ideal place for growth. I felt overworked and unappreciated. My director had a bad attitude and she was constantly shouting at and belittling her staff. Complaints that I made didn't go very far. It felt like a dead end. For a while I kept fighting it. I had goals of climbing the corporate ladder, earning more and buying more material things. Due to the climate though, I eventually had to ask myself, "Is this what you really want?" The answer was no. I had no love nor passion for the job. The treatment I received sometimes took a toll on me mentally and emotionally. I started to revisit my goals and think about my passion. I always loved reading and writing from the time I was a young child. I reconnected with this long-lost love in an effort to find myself and I haven't turned back since. I don't regret not achieving my original goal of climbing the corporate ladder because it wasn't for me. It was just a winding road taking me to where I am now, and I have made peace with that. Through that experience I learned to envision the best possible outcome without clinging to it for dear life. Let go and let flow. Let life unfold. Remember that childlike wonder that I spoke about? It comes in handy here. Don't be too rigid. If after all your hard work and optimism, something doesn't work out, maybe the timing isn't right. Maybe redirection is necessary. This is why it's so important to work on yourself and your energy. So that you're able to go inwards and return to stillness to get these messages that will guide you through. You don't know until you know.

Have Patience

I won't expand too much on this one at this point, since patience is a seed in itself that requires a detailed walkthrough. This will be covered in the next chapter. I will say that patience is an important part of faith. The two need to coexist. One will be weak without the other. If you don't have patience, you're not giving yourself time to build your faith. Patience in itself is a display of your faith. It says it's not here right now, but it will come if it is to come. If you don't have faith, you will get frustrated and discouraged easily. If you think that something is taking too long to come to you or if you're working hard and not seeing immediate rewards, you'll be tempted to walk away. Faith gives you the patience to help you grow, no matter how slow that growth seems at times. It takes you away from always expecting instant gratification. It keeps you peaceful and helps you to work through your frustrations when they do arise. I was once a very impatient person. For me, it was now or never. I eventually learned that I felt this way because my faith in myself was low, my faith in life was low, my faith in God and the universe was low. I didn't want to wait because I needed to see it now to believe it. If I put in a bit of work for something in the morning, I wanted to see the rewards by afternoon. If evening came without my rewards, I'd pretty much give up. I was robbing myself of the chance to see my life's true potential. I worked on my faith in order to grow my patience. And then I worked on my patience to grow my faith. I continue to work on both in order to strengthen them simultaneously.

ACTIVITY: 'Fear to Faith' Jar

How many times have you had something big or important coming up and fear crept in slowly until it filled the entire room (your mind)? Maybe you were about to start a new job. Maybe it was a new project at work. Maybe a baby was on the way. Maybe you were just thinking about your next move in life – whether personal or career-wise.

Many times, my fears kept me up late at night or interrupted my night rest. Even in my sleep, I'd dream about my fears. Reflecting on this made me come up with this activity to help soothe my fears. I invite you to try it.

- Get a clean jar.
- Choose an amount of money you can commit to putting in the jar whenever you feel fearful about something. I committed to one dollar.
- Whenever you feel fearful put your dollar (or whatever amount you choose) into the jar and visualize yourself letting your fears go. Imagine that you are placing the fear in the jar with the money.

- Repeat as necessary.

- Let the jar do the work. Imagine that the jar turns those fears into faith for you.

- Whenever you face and overcome your fear, return to the jar for the money that you accumulated.

- Treat yourself to whatever you can afford with your rewards of faith, even if it's just a scoop of ice cream or a pack of nuts. It's all about what your reward symbolizes.

For me, this activity doubled as an act of mindfulness. I stopped letting myself get carried away with my worries down the dark road of despair. Instead, I really imagined myself locking my fears in that jar when I closed the lid after placing the money into it. It reminded me to make a special effort to let my fearful thoughts go and just be present. If I couldn't do anything about whatever I was obsessing over in that moment, then what was the point of obsessing? It's easier said than done. It takes lots of practice. But you can get to a point where your fears don't constantly stifle you and lead you astray. You'll realize that you let go a little easier each time, or each few times. You'll never stop having fears altogether. The key is to take away fear's control over your thoughts, actions or inactions and habits. You have the power to do that.

Let Faith Take You Forward

I want you to make a promise to yourself to let faith take you forward from here on out. Believe in yourself like never before. Make peace with discomfort and the unknown. Be willing to put yourself out there and not be perfect. Be willing to mess up. Be willing to make changes as you go. Be willing to abandon it all and start fresh if you need to. Readjust your entire perspective where failure is concerned. Most of us see failure as trying something and not achieving the desired outcome. I want you to erase this definition of failure from your inner dictionary. From now on, when you try at something, if you learn something from it, acknowledge it as a pass and not a fail. It may not be the success that you expected, but it was indeed a success in its own right. It doesn't matter what you've learned. It can be as simple as, "I think I need to approach this challenge differently. Let me do more research and try something else" or "Maybe this isn't for me. I've realized that my goal has changed." As small as it seems, these are initial thoughts that lay the foundation for acts of bravery, once you make the next step. Go ahead and do the research that you promised you'd do. Go ahead and explore that new goal that you now want to achieve. Challenge yourself by leaning into the unknown without a guarantee that things will go exactly as you'd planned. Try one more time. Then one more time again. Take one more step. Then another one. This is the way to weave your way through life and discover all there is for you to see and to reap during this journey. So, you might ask, then what's the new definition of failure? Failure is the act of starving your faith and your true potential. It's ignoring that tiny voice that tells you to try something new. It's falling victim to your fears and letting them hold you hostage. Failure is playing it safe when you know within your heart that you'd like to take a risk. Once you move in faith, you won't experience failure.

Faith is taking the first step even when you don't see the whole staircase.

– Dr. Martin Luther King, Jr.

Patience

Patience - An ability or willingness to suppress restlessness or annoyance when confronted with delay *(Dictionary.com)*

Patience *(for the context of this book)* – Becoming acquainted with and understanding of the discomforts along the way as you strive to achieve a desired outcome *(Shakira Stuart)*

I slouched down on the ground

Hand gripping my chest

With furrowed brows

And my face masked by sweat

I always contemplate the end

When I can't control my breath

Heart thumping

Brain overheating

Because it's been in overdrive

Trying to get fearful thoughts to subside

1, 2, 3 - Breathe in

4, 5, 6 - Breathe out

I've repeated this exercise 5 times now

But it's getting no better

In fact, the panic's growing stronger

What they call anxiety

Feels like execution to me

But...

Just when I felt like I was out of luck

A soft voice in my head told me to look up

Reluctantly I obliged

Now I was staring up above wide eyed

Looking down at me was a clear blue sky

There was a stillness

One that I never knew could exist

It felt like peace

Perfection

Infinite bliss

As I got lost following a cloud

I heard the voice say, "Listen now."

A light, gentle whistle

Serenaded my ear

This was a sound

I've never before stopped to hear

The song of the wind

I could have been singing

But I was always going

Worried about the next thing

In my warped twisted mind

I was always running out of time

Now I was watching the leaves blow

Swaying nice and slow

Then I thought about how

They fall and bloom

With the changing seasons

Reminding me of my own transformation

Except that I'd always resist

I could only dream to be as graceful as this

Accepting growth when being watered

And embracing shedding for rebirth

When the water runs dry

And the days get hotter

There's never any urgency

Just an intuitive feeling

To let things be

As they should be

Now my heart rate was steady

And my breathing no longer heavy

As I took in the lesson nature taught me

I saw patience in nature

And in my nature, I saw patience

Once I let go of my resistance

And embraced the joy

Of being present

*- **Black Tea & Honey***

Patience in A Fast-Paced World

To date, patience has been one of my biggest struggles. I feel the tension and aches and pains in my body when I am resisting the present, worrying myself sick about a future I can't possibly predict, nor that I can even guarantee. The world that we live in doesn't make this any better. It's very fast-paced and full of shortcuts. People all over are trying to achieve something amazing in as little time as possible, putting in even less effort than time. "Lose 10 lbs. in just 2 weeks without exercise." "Turn your small business into a 6-figure earner in 1 month", "Get clear, flawless skin in 6 weeks using this simple face serum". There are so many tools available to us so that we can cut down on the time spent putting in work. This need for speed trickles into all areas of our lives. We choose fast food over making a quality meal in the kitchen. We pay extra for next-day or same-day delivery. We pay for the fastest internet speed that we can afford. We prefer to watch the movie over reading the book simply because the latter would take twice as long. While convenient, this has subconsciously taught us to expect everything as soon as possible. Once we can get something sooner, we go that route, often ignoring potential consequences.

Further to this, technology has given us the opportunity to be up close and personal, or so we think, in the lives of others. Generally, persons don't come forward with their struggles on social media. Instead, they show the best of their lives. People show off their fancy cars, beautiful houses, weekend getaways, trips to exotic places, dinner at expensive restaurants, perfect family moments, and the list goes on. Even if things aren't that great, "fake it 'til you make it" is a common theme on these platforms. People seldom get on social media and admit that they took out a loan in order to travel, or saved for 3 months to go to that new bar everyone has been raving about, or secretly dream of gathering the courage to break up with the partner that they always post because the relationship is actually toxic behind closed doors. We seldom get the full story in a social media post. Despite that fact, we compare their highlight reel to our everyday lives. This sometimes causes us to think that we are missing out on some fairytale. So, we impose deadlines on ourselves. We want to get things that we see other persons with and do the things that we see them doing, convincing ourselves that it will bring happiness. Other times, we aren't even able to pinpoint why we come up with some arbitrary deadlines for our goals. And if we don't achieve the goal by the intended time, we can't even identify a consequence in many cases, because there's none. I've heard it all. And for a long time, I subscribed to some of it. "I need to be married by 25." "I need to start a family by 27." "My business needs to be successful before I turn 30." "I need my own house by 35." "I need to be debt-free by the time I turn 50."

Hell, I even gave myself one of those deadlines when I began writing this book! "I need to have my book published by my 30th birthday" is what I kept telling myself over and over. The more I allowed the thought of the approaching deadline to haunt me, the less motivated and inspired I became, and the less work I put in, and the guiltier I felt. No surprise there! It was a constant downhill spiral for me, going in circles between feeling guiltier and doing less until I was doing absolutely nothing and feeling like a failure. That continued until I let go of the deadline that I placed on myself. I decided instead to respect the creative process and commit to doing a little each day. I also committed to not beating myself up if I skipped a day or two. I allowed myself to be flawed and to take my time because that's what this project deserved. My only promise to myself that I wasn't willing to compromise on, was that I'd keep trying. I was unwavering with that promise because I knew what writing this book meant to me. I knew how deeply I felt, and continue to feel, about taking the opportunity to share my gift of love, encouragement and communication through my words. Funny enough, when I allowed myself to relax with regards to the deadline, I became more productive. Isn't it amazing how the human mind works? I was also able to destroy a thought that I previously had – that patience is passive. It's far from. Patience is strength, willpower, calm, being present, faith and impulse control, all wrapped up in one beautiful bow.

There's Patience in Being Present

If you're wondering where to start with the practice of patience. I'd say being present is a great place to ground yourself. I want you to take a minute to contemplate. How many times were you fully immersed in whatever you were doing today? How many times did you give the task at hand your undivided attention? Is this something that you think you can achieve a few times daily? Or do you think you'd continue to be distracted by thoughts unrelated to that moment?

Admittedly, we spend lots of time with our bodies in one place, but our minds somewhere totally different. We are folding laundry and thinking about getting that meeting that we have in the morning over with. We are cooking food and dreading washing and cleaning up afterwards the entire time. We are driving and thinking about how long it's taking for our business to pick up and make more money. We are lying in bed to rest and thinking about that better life that we will be living 5 years from now. We constantly unintentionally rob ourselves of the present moment, often missing out on the richness and blessings right in front of us. How many times have you found yourself saying "I can't wait until..."? Start replacing that dialogue with "I'm patient for *whatever it is that you want to happen*" then rest in the present moment.

Our minds will wander from time to time regardless, that's part of its beauty. The issue with a wandering mind arises when our thoughts make us sad, anxious, depressed, unsettled and generally lower our vibration. This is the perfect time to return once again to your circle of control. When you're stuck in your head and it has changed your entire mood, interrupt that disruptive chatter by asking yourself if you can do something right now about that thing you're worrying about. If the answer is yes, then do something about it – after careful consideration, of course. If the answer is no, after you spend some time with what is bothering you, you have to work on letting it go. It makes no sense torturing yourself thinking about "would" "should" and "could". That hypothetical monster can eat you alive if you let it. Sometimes, the best thing that you can do is let it all go and give your mind some rest.

Life is not about racing to a finish line. The truth is that the finish line is death. Each day that we wake up is a step closer to the finish line. So why rush it? Don't you want to enjoy as many of the days that you're given as possible? Why do you think that you have to choose between being happy now or being happy later? Or working hard or enjoying rest and relaxation? What if I told you that it was possible to do both? What if I told you that you deserve it all? You deserve to be happy now and happy later. You deserve to enjoy life while you work on your goals. You don't have to live in an extreme and completely sacrifice joy now in hopes of feeling joyful later. Trying to magically jump, or even work your way to a place where your life is perfect is actually the perfect way to waste your life. You'll always be chasing something new. There will always be another goal to achieve. Then you're like a hamster on a wheel, just going and going until time's up.

Instead of trying to find the perfect moment, find perfection in every moment. Otherwise, you'll be disappointed to find out that this perfect moment in this perfect place that you were working towards doesn't really exist. The beauty, luxury and joy that you think you'll find in the destination, actually resides in the journey. That beauty, luxury and joy is called life. It's up to you to see it for what it is. With that said, appreciate where you're at and embrace what you've achieved so far. Sometimes, just BE. Fully immerse yourself in the moment. Stop and smell a flower. Lie down at the beach and stare at the sky. Take a long walk and get lost in the scenery. Take a break, or maybe a few of them. Treat yourself as you are now. You deserve it. This way, you will be too deeply engrossed in the present to be impatiently obsessing about what will happen next and how the future will go.

ACTIVITY: The Practice of Presence

The next time that you are doing a mundane task like sweeping the house, doing the dishes or folding laundry, I want you to monitor your thoughts. Be the observer of your thoughts. I want you to be consciously aware of what you're thinking and how these thoughts are making you feel. Maybe you're worried about a loved one who is ill, and it has you sad. Maybe you're thinking about a fight you had with your mom the day before and you're still very angry and resentful. Whatever the thoughts are, just be aware of them. Try not to judge yourself for them. Journal your thoughts after you complete the activity.

The next time you have to do the same mundane task, I want you to do your best to remain present. If you're doing the dishes, focus on the suds that the dishwashing liquid creates, feel the temperature of the water as it runs on your hands, look at the dishes gradually going from dirty to clean as you continue to wash them. Every time your mind tries to take you somewhere else, acknowledge it and then gently bring it back to the task. It doesn't matter how many times you get distracted. This is not a test, just an exercise in mindfulness and being present. Once you've completed the exercise, journal how it went and how you felt. Did being present and immersed in your activity calm you in any way? Did it bore you? Was it easy or difficult? There are no right or wrong answers.

The above exercise can be very helpful when you find yourself completely distracted by something that is making you anxious or depressed. Reroute your focus to give your mind a short break and see how it impacts how you feel.

There's Patience in Planning

Take some time to once again reflect on your goals. Think about all the things that you'd like to accomplish in this lifetime. All the things you're willing to work towards. Most of us have a big and fruitful life dreamed up. The reality is, you won't just wake up suddenly with everything in your lap. It's a process and good things take time. Great things take even longer. Usually, the bigger the dream, the more steps you'll have to take, the more sacrifices you'll have to make and the more time you'll have to wait. So really, getting acquainted with patience will make it a bit easier. But before it gets easier, it gets harder, because embracing and becoming one with patience is, in itself, a very daunting task.

Planning and executing are acts that separate the dreamer from the goal getter. For the goal getters, before you go anywhere you should have an idea of what it's going to take to get there. You should also be open to receiving teachable moments that you did not foresee. With that in mind, you plan the pathway to your goals. Consider the tasks you must complete, the habits you must build, the person you must become, the things you must put in place –

they are all very important. Your dedication to planning is a demonstration of your patience and those unforeseen teachable moments help you to build your patience even more.

Let's use a farmer as an example. The farmer's goal is to harvest and sell his crops. He doesn't just buy some seeds and throw them onto the soil then never look back until a few weeks later when he's expecting the crops to be ready. Not a good farmer, anyway! A good farmer prepares the land and researches the work he'd have to put in to grow the particular seedlings that he chose. He also maintains the land as the crops grow. He's watering the soil and the crops, pulling up weeds and getting rid of pests so that he gives his crops the optimum environment to grow. A great farmer is even willing to repeat this entire process from the beginning even if he wasn't successful the first time around. Let's say that some thieves come by and steal most of his crops just before he gets the chance to harvest. Cue the teachable moment! He realizes that he can better protect his land going forward and puts security measures in place. Without patience, he would walk away from that venture after investing so much time, effort and money, only to be robbed unfairly. Knowledge and willpower tell him that he can plan a little better and do it all again for the rewards to come. Patience helps him to see the process through once again. Of course, he went through feelings of anger, disappointment and sadness due to what happened. Patience told him to try again despite experiencing these feelings. Sometimes when things don't go your way and you are dwelling on it, it is actually impatience arising. Things didn't go your way in that instance. It doesn't mean that they won't ever go your way. Patience helps you to renew the plan and return to the path. Without patience, frustration and disappointment can easily cloud your judgement and cause you to quit prematurely. Patience sits with you as you create the plan and follow through with it, tweaking it as necessary instead of being permanently discouraged by any challenges that arise.

My Patience Project

At the beginning of 2020, one of my goals for that year was to make something that I can sell. I wanted to embrace my creative side, while also offering something to others that I put my love and effort into. By this time, I was very serious about my personal and professional development, so that same month (January) I had already signed up for a jewelry making class. No one else signed up at the time, so the teacher asked me if I was okay with a one-on-one class and of course I said yes! I went into the class excited because I had already planned out how things would go. I tend to do a lot of daydreaming. The course was 6 weeks long – 2 hours each Saturday and I was given homework after each class. My teacher was very skillful and knowledgeable in the field, but more importantly, she was kind, nurturing and extremely patient. At some point during the first class, I remember jokingly telling her that I didn't know how I'd get along with the craft since I was naturally impatient. I also remember her telling me in a very calm voice with a gentle smile, "Just pray about it."

I didn't take her advice in that moment. But eventually I had to. Jewelry-making really tested and strengthened my patience. The real work started after the course was over and the teacher let go of my hand. I expected to be a pro after that 6 weeks, so of course, there was a multitude of resistance and impatience as I tried and failed at various designs. That's when I realized that I needed to be patient if I wanted to allow myself to get better at the craft. That's also when I started to pray for patience each morning. Only then did I begin to practice more, watch tutorials and read "how-to" blogs in order to increase my knowledge and commit to trying again and again. Lots of materials ended up in the waste bin after experiments went wrong, but I'd never call it wastage because I had to do it to see where I was going wrong and how to improve next time around.

My favourite patience project to date is making waist beads. Stringing 2mm-4mm beads one by one onto a string measuring 30-37" long, sometimes even longer. I even got creative and experimented with extravagant designs with double strands or all kinds of loops and hoops. Sometimes, I'd be sitting making an intricate design for hours, all the while completely enamored with the beauty of the process. There were also times when I was almost finished with a strand and while checking the measurement, my finger slipped and almost all the beads slid off the string and scattered all over the floor. The first time it happened I almost cried as I watched all my hard work slide out of my hand and disappear within a few seconds. These incidents did not come without a lesson though. I learned (the hard way) how to properly secure the unfinished waist beads before checking the measurement. Knowing how far I came, my pride whenever I look at my finished product is unmatched. No one knows as well as I do the patience that I had to build to see a process like that through. Now, stringing waist beads isn't a race to finish for me. It has become quite therapeutic.

ACTIVITY: Your Patience Project

Now, I want you to come up with your own patience project. Think about a hobby or activity that you'd like to try or pick back up if you can make space for it in your life right now. I know that we are all very busy. It can be a 1000-piece puzzle, starting your own home garden, rollerblading or yoga. Or think about something that will help you with your professional development. Maybe there's a book that you can read or a course that you can take. Maybe you can learn or brush up on a foreign language.

After coming up with your chosen project, take the following steps:

- Decide on the amount of time that you can commit to your Patience Project each day. It can be as little as 10-15 minutes. The idea is to do a little each day. Make your target manageable and realistic.

- Let go of any deadlines that you may feel inclined to place on this project. There are none. The idea is to patiently watch your progress. Little progress is still progress.

- Whenever you get frustrated or feel like you should be further along, read the above.

- Be forgiving and graceful with yourself if you skip a day or 2. Doubling up to make up for the time lost is not necessary, but you can do it if you want to. For example, if you miss two 15-minute sessions, you can choose to pick back up as normal or do two 15-minute sessions for the next 2 days to make up for the sessions missed.

- Remain mindful of the progress that you made by doing a little each day.

I usually use the Patience Project for reading. I commit to reading 15-20 minutes each morning. Depending on the length of the book, it can take a week to several weeks to finish. Detaching from a deadline makes reading more enjoyable and I am able to take in a little information each time and thirst for more, as opposed to trying to cram it all in in a few hours.

Whatever you do, enjoy your Patience Project and open yourself up to applying this method to other areas of your life. Ironically, you need patience (with yourself) to build patience. Don't be discouraged if it doesn't feel like a walk in the park. Like most things, it will get easier with practice.

There's Patience in Finding Purpose

Have you ever asked yourself "What's the purpose of my life?" or "Why am I here?" I've asked myself this question many times, especially in recent years. I think that we all have a purpose in this life. We tend to assign weight and levels of importance to people's purpose. But really, all are important. It doesn't matter HOW important. Don't worry if you're not entirely sure of your purpose right now. You must be purposeful to find your purpose; I like to say. Basically, the more open you become to exploring in order to find your purpose, the closer you will get to putting the puzzle pieces together. You have to want to know your purpose. That's the first step. The next step is getting acquainted with faith and patience. Trust that you'll find your purpose. Trust that you'll know when you find it. Trust that it is not something that you can possibly rush or fast track. Trust that it will happen in divine timing.

That's a lot of trust that you have to put out there. You can't build that trust without patience. It makes no sense putting pressure on yourself to find your purpose. Naturally, pressure, tight deadlines, and wanting it now will make you impatient. I believe that finding your purpose is a very intuitive process. You'll know when you know. Until then, commit to patiently unraveling all your layers, getting to know yourself better and growing in whatever areas you can. At your core, you'll discover your purpose, so this is the best way to prepare. It is a long road. You won't get there overnight or in a few nights, for that matter. If you try to rush it, you might see signs where there are none, misinterpret information and fall further away from purpose. Then, it would take even longer to discover. If your purpose is heavy on your mind at any time, rest knowing that you'll figure it out exactly when you're meant to do so.

Discipline

Discipline - An activity, exercise, or regimen that develops or improves a skill; training *(Dictionary.com)*

Self-Discipline - The ability to control one's feelings and overcome one's weaknesses; the ability to pursue what one thinks is right despite temptations to abandon it *(Lexico Online Dictionary)*

Self-Discipline *(for the context of this book)* – Commitment, focus and persistence in order to achieve a set of tasks or goals, despite the challenges that arise *(Shakira Stuart)*

Slow and steady

Day by day

I make my way

Forward

Upward

Onward

I never backslide

The lessons I've learned

The knowledge I've gained

Can never be erased

From my mind

So even on the days

That I feel totally stuck

Or have to start over again

I know I've given

The best of me yet

And I'll become better

As long as I commit

To the journey

To the path

To purpose

Most days I feel like a soldier

Armoured in wisdom

With experience as my weapon

Ready to face whatever

Life may throw my way

Knowing that I'm a conqueror

A fighter

A brave heart

As I set eyes on another day

I work hard

But more importantly

I rest

I know when to honour

Time to unwind

And reflect

Time to be

Holds as much importance as

Time to do

And time to achieve

For nothing in nature

Blooms all year

So why would I dare

Reject the very nature

Of my own existence

I've let go and let flow

Cutting ties with resistance

Sometimes I'm a butterfly

Other times I'm a caterpillar

And in between

I'm the cocoon

At all times I'm graceful

With each cycle I go through

And at all times I'm mindful

To be disciplined

In my thoughts

My habits

And my speech

As I manifest

The person

I'm meant to be

*- **Black Tea & Honey***

The Vilification of Discipline

Generally, there's quite an intimidating connotation of what discipline looks like. The narrative that is pushed is one of torture, suffering and becoming one with misery by working yourself incessantly, all with the objective of achieving your goals. Just step onto social media and you will see it in no time. "No days off" "Team no sleep" and "Late nights, early mornings" are just a few of the terms thrown around to symbolize hard work and seriousness about achieving goals. Often, the goal is to get rich. So many people still believe that this is the solution to all of life's problems. So, they subscribe to the "grind culture" of get rich or die trying. Actor, businessman, and former stand-up comedian Steve Harvey once said, "Rich people don't sleep eight hours a day." And one of the richest men in the world, Bill Gates said, "I never took a day off in my twenties. Not one." To be fair, Gates did follow up by saying that he didn't recommend this method as most people wouldn't enjoy it. Though he gave that piece of advice discrediting his method, some people might see it as somewhat of a challenge. "Oh, you're saying that you could handle it, but I can't? Let me prove otherwise." Because the fact still remains that Steve Harvey, Bill Gates and many others got rich by living that way, so it is normal for persons to seek to imitate them in an effort to reach success too. This is how an unhealthy lifestyle laser focused on goals is born. Burn out is worn as a badge of honour. Pushing yourself past the limit is seen as true drive and discipline. Symptoms of anxiety and depression are ignored. Taking a break to honour rest and relaxation is seen as slacking off. Taking time to recharge is considered time wasted. And there's an immense guilt that accompanies any moment of unproductivity. Furthermore, productivity becomes a measurement of self-worth. What if I told you that discipline doesn't have to look like this? What if I told you that discipline is not a method of torture and punishment?

The True Image of Discipline

I've always admired persons who are consistent with exercise. Seeing them continue to commit to a healthy lifestyle. Seeing them workout 3 to 4 days a week religiously, sometimes more often. Although I deeply admired them, a small part of me always wondered how they could subject themselves to such torture. It seemed like torture in my eyes because it felt like torture for me when I tried to commit to doing it. Three to four weeks in and I was over it and ready to return to "normal". Normal for me looked like no exercise at all, and lots of snacks. Unconsciously, that's a habit that I spent years building. Normal varies from person to person. The same way I was wondering how a "gym rat" could live like that, they were probably wondering the same about me. This realization hit home for me when I was in conversation with my personal trainer. It was my umpteenth attempt at cleaning up my act and becoming more health conscious. I decided on one-on-one personal training to help me to establish a solid routine. A scheduled workout 3 days a week under my trainer's watchful eye, in addition to a meal plan and progress checks. One day, during a workout, I was in the middle of a sit-up when I exclaimed that I'd love a pack of Doritos. He laughed and said that he was never a "snacker". I never identified with that type, but curiosity pushed me to ask a question. "How did you become so disciplined about your workout regime and eating habits?" He replied without a second thought, "Because I love it." Of course, I asked him to elaborate and when he broke it down it blew my mind. He explained that he loves his body and seeing it grow and become stronger the more work he puts in. Seeing and feeling the results brought him joy. Challenging himself in the gym and seeing his body gradually adapt was fascinating. Feeling healthy, energetic and powerful was like a drug to him. These feelings almost always beat the feeling to sleep in and skip gym or spend the night eating ice cream and binge-watching his favourite show. And when he slipped up, he was able to get back on track because he was invested. He knew his "why" and he was committed to it.

It suddenly made sense to me. Discipline will always be a challenge, but it becomes more manageable when your heart is in it. You have to have a deep desire to see it through and achieve the goal. This is why intention is so important. Discipline isn't about punishing yourself to obtain something you think you should have. It's about going the extra mile to manifest something that you're passionate about. It is deeply personal. This is why you can only follow the advice of others to a certain extent. Get in touch with what's important to you and what works for you.

After exploring the process of discipline, I realized something else equally important. Discipline doesn't mean never slipping up nor mentally beating up yourself unmercifully when you do. It means getting right back on track after you slip up. It means understanding that progress doesn't always look the same nor is it linear. It means letting go of that slip up and moving forward. Because when you know your "why" your discipline isn't permanently shaken that easily. You get back on track time and time again. You know that rest is important if you want to give of your best. You can be disciplined and well-rested too! It's called balance. You work towards building habits that you can actually sustain without feeling fatigued or burnt out in a few weeks or months. The aim is to build long-term self-discipline that doesn't involve intense suffering.

The Gradual Nature of Discipline

Discipline is a bit of a paradox. I say this because it takes discipline to build discipline. Discipline is needed to build habits. But discipline is also a habit in itself that needs to be built. If your actions are usually based on impulsive thoughts, your emotions or instant gratification, then building discipline will be more difficult. You'll have to train your mind to control impulses by thinking about situations deeply before deciding to act. In general, you won't just wake up as a disciplined person. It's a step-by-step program and many only speak on the last few steps. For example, the general consensus is you should exercise three times a week on average. Someone that has never had a steady exercise routine would most likely find it difficult to commit to this straight off the bat. Of course, with the initial excitement and motivation, they may be able to maintain this routine for a few weeks. However, when the motivation runs out and they hit a plateau, they may revert to old habits. Instead, it might be better for them to commit to two 20-minute workouts per week and then gradually increase. This is how a life-long sustainable habit is built. The results may be slower to come, but they also have a greater chance of lasting longer. Think about the number of persons that try all kinds of diets and weight loss programs, losing a significant amount of weight in a short period of time and then packing it right back on some weeks or months later, only to repeat the process all over again. How willing would you be to commit to the longer route in order to build a lasting habit? Start small and build your discipline as you build your habit, whether it is exercise, studying, working on a project or working on your personal development.

I witnessed firsthand the gradual progression of discipline when I reflected on my meditation journey. I started out some time in 2018. I simply found videos on YouTube and did guided meditations occasionally as a way to help calm my anxiety. I then took an 8-week course in meditation theory and practice. It was during this time that I developed a deeper understanding and appreciation of meditation. I learned different techniques that I could try, and I also got some pointers to help me to become more mindful and present. It was through this love for what I learned that I gradually and naturally started meditating more often. I decided to commit to morning meditations to set the tone for the day. Many times, I fell asleep during meditation or I was completely restless, but something about the practice always made me feel very calm. There were times that I skipped a few days of meditation. Eventually I'd feel a desire to meditate and I would start back. No judgement. No guilt. I'd just move forward. For me, it never felt forced and I didn't heavily scrutinize my progress, unlike many other things in my life. I just... meditated. It helped that I read many books over time that further emphasized the benefits of meditation and mindfulness. I just took in the knowledge and went with the flow. Now? I meditate almost every morning. It has become a ritual for me and if I miss a day, I feel as though I forgot to do something important. I won't claim to be a guru. I still doze off during meditations from time to time. I still also feel restless from time to time. But every morning I show up and I try. And the day that I think I might need to break for whatever compelling reason, I will. Overall, it's not something that I can see myself walking away from permanently because it has become a part of me. I've also had way less bad days due to anxiety and overthinking as a result of meditation and mindfulness practices. That's what discipline achieves.

Building Discipline

We established that discipline is a habit that takes a while to build. Most habits take a while, even bad ones. Think of an alcoholic. It's very unlikely that they started off drinking all night until they passed out. Maybe it started with a few drinks every payday to ease the stress. Maybe as life got more challenging, they gradually resorted to alcohol as a way to escape their reality. Maybe it went from weekend drinking only to drinking every night. This detrimental habit was established over a period of time. We all have bad habits. It may not be as destructive as alcohol, but maybe something we should cut back on to improve the quality of our lives. Sometimes, we look at our bad habit and wonder, "How did I get here?" Well, if you reflect, you will see exactly how you gradually got to that point over time. But there's a lesson in reflecting on our bad habits. It shows that we are all capable of creating new habits in our lives. We get to choose whether or not these habits will contribute positively to our growth and wellbeing.

ACTIVITY: Break A Habit, Build A Habit

I challenge you to think of one habit you'd like to break and one new habit you'd like to create to replace the old one. It doesn't have to be anything too extreme. It could be as simple as cutting down on junk food and instead snacking on fruit, protein bars or healthy shakes.

Set an Intention – Write down what you'd like to accomplish. This is your official commitment to yourself. Also note down your "why". This part is important for you to refer to when you feel discouraged. Once you've written everything down, read it out loud. Put it out into the universe. Your statement can look like *"I commit to eating less junk food and having healthy snacks as a replacement. My body is my home and I want to take care of it so that I am healthier and have more energy to achieve my other life goals."*

Make A Plan – How will you achieve your goal? What steps will you need to take? What are you going to do, when are you going to do it and how often? Using the example of replacing junk food with healthy snacks, your plan can look like this.

- *Create a shopping list*
- *Go to the supermarket over the weekend*
- *Clear out junk food; if it's not there I can't eat it*
- *Make sure to eat a solid breakfast, lunch and dinner*
- *Drink enough water*
- *Drink a cup of water before my healthy snack*
- *Have 2 healthy snacks per day*

Complete the Action – This is where your strength and willpower have to come in. Writing the intention and the plan is easy in comparison to this step. You actually have to follow through with your plan. Try your best not to put it off nor make excuses. If it's important to you, you'll do it.

Build A Habit – The website www.healthline.com referred to a 2009 study published in the European Journal of Social Psychology, concluding that it takes 18 to 254 days for a person to form a new habit. The study's findings also indicated that on average it takes 66 days for a new behaviour to become automatic. In any case, 18 to 254 days is a pretty big range. In building your habit, don't be concerned with the number of days it may take. You won't know until your habit is established. Instead, focus on repeating the action/s needed to build your habit each day. Take it one day at a time and show up as best as you can each day.

Make It A Ritual – As you build your habit, over time it might become second nature. You'll eventually be grabbing for that apple without thinking, instead of craving a piece of candy. While this is great, it is also important to be present with each action and remember your "why". You create a ritual by remaining intentional in your actions and what you want to achieve through completing them.

Handling Roadblocks to Discipline

Even with all the related information and knowledge under your belt, discipline will still be challenging. It will not always go smoothly, but by now you should see that that is a recurring theme when it comes to self-transformation on a whole. The path from knowing what to do to consistently doing it is a long and winding one. People often underestimate how much willpower it takes to be disciplined. Your mind will absolutely fight you when you're trying to break old habits and create new ones. You will be tempted to give up for good at times when you fall off. Sometimes your "why" won't even offer you the motivation that you need. This is the perfect time to reflect on all the other seeds of self-transformation. Set aside some time alone and engage in quiet reflection. Bring your awareness to how you feel in that moment, the things around you, and your current circumstance. Accept that you've hit a stumbling block and accept the feelings of frustration and discouragement that you're currently facing. Accept that the discomfort is sometimes overwhelming. But although you've hit a stumbling block, I'm sure that you've still achieved something. Even if it was one single day of discipline. That still counts. Congratulate yourself and show gratitude for what you've done. Think about all the other things that you can feel grateful for – maybe a friend that agreed to be your accountability buddy, maybe an encouraging partner or a random person that helped you along the way at some point. Close your eyes and feel the gratitude deeply.

After sitting with gratitude for some time, show yourself some love.

You might feel low and as though you don't deserve it because you haven't been disciplined enough to achieve your goal. But you still have time and maybe a break was needed anyway. No matter how much we do, we usually think that we can do a little more. So, it's okay if you're feeling like you didn't do enough so far. Still show yourself some love. Treat yourself to an off day. Do something that you'll enjoy. This is a way to show yourself unconditional love. Go out of your way to lift your spirits, like you would a friend in the same circumstance. You wouldn't berate them about what they should or could have done. You'd embrace them with loving kindness because you want them to feel better and get back on their feet. Want the same for yourself. Act accordingly. After your self-loving moment and cultivating a calmer spirit, reflect on faith and patience together. If these two seeds aren't properly fertilized, they can create huge stumbling blocks. Do you still believe in yourself and your abilities? Did you ever? Do you really think you can achieve your goals? Does it truly feel possible to you? If you're answering in the affirmative to all these questions, then maybe it is impatience that's holding you back. Maybe you're tired of not seeing real results for the efforts that you've put in. Or maybe you haven't been patient enough to even put in real effort. Rate your patience from 1 to 10 at this time. Are you clinging to an unrealistic deadline? Are you refusing to put in the work because it seems like too much? Are you just fed up? Why? Pour your heart out. Be completely honest with yourself. Do it as though your future depends on it – because it does. Work on renewing your faith and your patience. Once you're in a better place, revisit your plan for building discipline. Action it again.

The key to this entire process is going slowly. Take your time with each seed. You can repeat it again if you still feel like you need to dig deeper. Or you can take a break from everything and return later. Sometimes rest is all we need to feel renewed and ready to conquer the challenges of life once again.

Water Your Seeds,

Pull the Weeds

Amongst all living creatures on Earth, humans are the only ones who can make deliberate choices about the direction that they'd like their lives to go in and to become who they envision. Humans have the ability to think and be the awareness behind those thoughts. Our thoughts, consciousness and behaviours are way more complex than any other species. Why not make full use of this power? Why not explore all the wonders of being human?

Remember the plot of land that I mentioned in the introduction? I spoke about watering the seeds so that you can grow and produce the crops to feed yourself and your loved ones. Now that you've explored each of the seeds that you need to plant for your self-transformation, it's important to remember that you need to keep watering and nurturing these seeds as long as you want to reap the rewards. There's an old Bajan saying, "You reap what you sow." If you sow potatoes, you can't possibly reap eddoes. Similarly, if you sow unappreciation, fear and hate, you can't reap gratitude, faith and love. It's impossible. You have to keep replanting what you'd like to reap as you go through life. It has to be consciously and intentionally done. Further to that, you have to pay special attention to your crops along the way. Keep watering them. Look out for weeds. Weeds will always grow from time to time. It's your job to make sure that they don't take over your garden. Work on pulling those weeds as soon as you see them. And the same way that you'll have to keep watering your crops, you'll have to keep pulling weeds. Eventually, the job will get a little easier as you build expertise in dealing with your crops and keeping the weeds at bay. It's called learning life lessons and applying those lessons going forward.

At times, you will be tried and tested immensely. This is when you'll want to walk away from your garden most. This is also when you should be more attentive to your garden. In other words, there will be trials and tribulations. When you ask and pray for something of great value, you have to prove that you really want it. Keep taking another step forward and showing up another day. Even while you rest, think of your garden. Send it love and give thanks. As small as this act may seem, it puts positive energy and intention into your garden and by extension, the universe. When things get overwhelming, take a look at what you created from a bare plot of land, from a blank canvas. The road ahead always seems like a long one. The road traveled was long too, but you still made it this far. That's admirable.

The Fruit of Your Labour

As you go deeper into your practices for growth and self-transformation, you're guaranteed to see certain results. Things that used to trouble you deeply will start to lose their power. You will no longer be paralyzed and silenced by fear. You will have the tools to work through those fears, no matter how long it may take. You'll become a more relaxed, optimistic and open-hearted person. You'll rest more easily knowing that you're trying your best, considering that your best will look different at different times depending on your circumstance. You'll also see opportunities for further growth in the challenges that you face. Overall, you will build a deeper connection with and understanding of yourself. This is key to showing up as your best and most authentic self each moment. As you embody this person, you'll begin to see beauty and joy in simple day-to-day things in life. Furthermore, you will take advantage of more opportunities to create your own joy where possible.

Your relationship with others will also change. It will happen like a domino effect. Remember that positive thought and positive action together don't only reap positive results in your life, but also in the lives of those you influence. As you become a safe space for yourself, you also become one for others. You will be more compassionate, loving and understanding towards others. You will take things less personally as you see that other persons are just working through their particular stage of being a human. You will be able to recognize when someone tries to project their own fear, insecurity or anger onto you. Someone that's always mean to you, is clearly unhappy with themselves. Instead of returning their energy, you will extend compassion and sympathy, knowing that they are acting out because they are suffering. And you are not responsible for that suffering. You'll also extend these same feelings for persons "stuck in their ways" because you're experiencing first-hand how difficult and scary self-transformation can be. Even persons that are hurting badly, will be able to see the light in you and it might just encourage them to begin their healing too. You'll also attract more persons who are on their own self-transformation journey. Don't lower your frequency to match energies when someone is engaging in negative action towards you. Instead, stand in your light. Be the type of person you want to attract. This is how you find your tribe.

As you change, your circle and circumstances will change too. It's okay to mourn aspects of your old life as you step into and celebrate your new one.

A Final Word of Insight

Whatever you do and wherever you go, make sure that you are staying true to you. This world is a busy one, sometimes very chaotic, so it's easy to get lost. Remember that home is always inside of you. Cut off the distractions, get really quiet, put your hand over your chest and as you feel your heartbeat, listen to your heart too. When you're feeling lost, let it show you the way. Trust your intuition to show you the next move. Meditate, talk to God, journal to yourself or to the universe, whatever you feel comfortable doing to help you explore your feelings. It's about you and what resonates with you. There's no one right way to do this thing called life. You're going to figure it out just like you always have. I promise you.

Cheers to you, your beautiful alter ego that was birthed and your highest self, who's coming to life in this very moment!

Every night I close my eyes

And recite a prayer

That has become my guide

"May I practice awareness

Firstly, of self

And those around me

May I welcome acceptance

Of all that is

And all that will be

May I be grateful

In every circumstance

Let that feeling propel me forward

As it helps me to understand

That gratitude is a tool

To embrace the present moment

And manifest a brighter future too

May love become one with me

May I show it through

Kindness, compassion and empathy

May I lean into faith

Throughout this journey

May I be patient

With myself

And each situation before me

And may I be disciplined

Letting no challenge deter me

So it is written

So it shall be"

- Black Tea & Honey

About The Author

Shakira Stuart
Author, Self-Love Advocate

Of all the languages in the world, love is the most powerful. Pure, unconditional, intentional love. I strive to practice, speak and teach this language daily in all aspects of my life.

From the time I was a young child, I yearned to feel loved. I chased acceptance and praise through my academic achievements since I was naturally gifted in that area. I felt as though I needed to earn love from family and friends by being outstanding in some way. I did not believe that I could simply be loved just as I was. This subconscious burden accompanied me all the way into adulthood, often weighing me down, especially in romantic relationships. For a long time, I couldn't pinpoint the source of the heaviness that I felt.

It is through adversity that I slowly began to see what I'd call "the light" and actively started to focus on healing and unlearning self-defeating beliefs. This is where immense, unconditional love for self, and then for others, came into play. I also delved deeply into my spirituality. The healing chapter of my journey has been so profound and impactful for me, that I felt like I had to share my story to encourage and guide others in their own unique path to a healed and healthy soul. Through this realization, I reacquainted myself with the pen and fell in love with writing all over again. Taking back up this childhood hobby truly awakened me. In essence, it is through my healing that I discovered my purpose. At my core, I was always a writer and perhaps it has always been my calling.

Currently, I share my stories and life lessons on my free online blog www.blackteaandhoney.blog under the pen name Black Tea & Honey. This book is my first of many to come. I also make jewelry, another creative outlet that I thoroughly enjoy. Creating is my passion and I hope to create positive and uplifting thoughts in the minds of everyone that I reach during my earthly journey.

Always with gratitude.

Shakira Stuart